JOURNEYMAN ELECTRICIAN PRACTICE EXAM

Theory • Code • Calculations

Suitable for all electrical exams based on the NEC®, such as: AMP, ICC, Local/State Examining Boards, Pearson VUE, Prometric, Prov, PSI, NASCLA

BASED ON THE
2020 NEC®

NOTICE TO THE READER

The text and commentary in this book is the author's interpretation of the 2020 Edition of NFPA 70®, the National Electrical Code®. It shall not be considered an endorsement of or the official position of the NFPA® or any of its committees, nor relied upon as a formal interpretation of the meaning or intent of any specific provision or provisions of the 2020 edition of NFPA 70, National Electrical Code.

The publisher does not warrant or guarantee any of the products described herein or perform any independent analysis in connection with any of the product information contained herein. The publisher does not assume, and expressly disclaims, any obligation to obtain and include information other than that provided to it by the manufacturer.

The reader is expressly warned to consider and adopt all safety precautions and applicable federal, state, and local laws and regulations. By following the instructions contained herein, the reader willingly assumes all risks in connection with such instructions.

Mike Holt Enterprises disclaims liability for any personal injury, property or other damages of any nature whatsoever, whether special, indirect, consequential or compensatory, directly or indirectly resulting from the use of this material. The reader is responsible for relying on his or her personal independent judgment in determining safety and appropriate actions in all circumstances.

The publisher makes no representation or warranties of any kind, including but not limited to, the warranties of fitness for particular purpose or merchantability, nor are any such representations implied with respect to the material set forth herein, and the publisher takes no responsibility with respect to such material. The publisher shall not be liable for any special, consequential, or exemplary damages resulting, in whole or part, from the reader's use of, or reliance upon, this material.

Mike Holt's Journeyman Electrician Practice Exam, based on the 2020 NEC®

Second Printing: October 2020

Author: Mike Holt
Cover Design: Bryan Burch
Layout Design and Typesetting: Cathleen Kwas

COPYRIGHT © 2020 Charles Michael Holt
ISBN 978-0-9992038-8-0

Produced and Printed in the USA

All rights reserved. No part of this work covered by the copyright hereon may be reproduced or used in any form or by any means graphic, electronic, or mechanical, including photocopying, recording, taping, or information storage and retrieval systems without the written permission of the publisher. You can request permission to use material from this text by e-mailing Info@MikeHolt.com.

For more information, call 888.NEC.CODE (632.2633), or e-mail Info@MikeHolt.com.

NEC®, NFPA 70®, NFPA 70E® and National Electrical Code® are registered trademarks of the National Fire Protection Association.

 This logo is a registered trademark of Mike Holt Enterprises, Inc.

If you are an instructor and would like to request an examination copy of this or other Mike Holt Publications:

Call: 888.NEC.CODE (632.2633) • Fax: 352.360.0983

E-mail: Info@MikeHolt.com • Visit: www.MikeHolt.com/Instructors

You can download a sample PDF of all our publications by visiting www.MikeHolt.com/products.

I dedicate this book to the
Lord Jesus Christ, *my mentor and teacher.*
Proverbs 16:3

"For All Your Electrical Training Needs"

www.MikeHolt.com

We Care...

Since the day we started our business over 40 years ago, we have been working hard to produce products that get results, and to help individuals in their pursuit of learning how to be successful in this exciting industry. I have built my business on the idea that customers come first, and that everyone on my team will do everything they possibly can to take care of you. I want you to know that we value you, and are honored that you have chosen us to be your partner in electrical training.

I believe that you are the future of this industry and that it is you who will make the difference in years to come. My goal is to share with you everything that I know and to encourage you to pursue your education on a continuous basis. I hope that not only will you learn theory, code, calculations or how to pass an exam, but that in the process you will become the expert in the field and the person who others know to trust.

We are dedicated to providing quality electrical training that will help you take your skills to the next level and we genuinely care about you. Thanks for choosing Mike Holt Enterprises for your electrical training needs.

God bless and much success,

Exam Preparation | Continuing Education | Apprenticeship Products | In-House Training | & more

"...as for me and my house, we will serve the Lord." [Joshua 24:15]

TABLE OF CONTENTS

About the Author vi

Practice Exam Instructions vii

Part 1—Basic Electrical Theory

Electrical Theory Exam (4 Hours) 1

Electrical Theory Answer Key 29

Electrical Theory Answer Sheet 51

Part 2—*National Electrical Code*®

National Electrical Code Exam (4 Hours) 11

National Electrical Code Answer Key 33

National Electrical Code Answer Sheet 53

Part 3—Electrical Calculations

Electrical Calculations Exam (6 Hours) 21

Electrical Calculations Answer Key 35

Electrical Calculations Answer Sheet 55

ABOUT THE AUTHOR

Mike Holt—Author

Founder and President
Mike Holt Enterprises

Mike Holt is an author, businessman, educator, speaker, publisher and *National Electrical Code* expert. He has written hundreds of electrical training books and articles, founded three successful businesses, and has taught thousands of electrical *Code* seminars across the U.S. and internationally. His electrical training courses have set the standard for trade education, enabling electrical professionals across the country to take their careers to the next level.

Mike's approach to electrical training is based on his own experience as an electrician, contractor, inspector and teacher. Because of his struggles in his early education, he's never lost sight of how hard it can be for students who are intimidated by school, by their own feelings towards learning, or by the complexity of the *NEC*. As a result of that, he's mastered the art of explaining complicated concepts in a straightforward and direct style. He's always felt a responsibility to his students and to the electrical industry to provide education beyond the scope of just passing an exam. This commitment, coupled with the lessons he learned at the University of Miami's MBA program, have helped him build one of the largest electrical training and publishing companies in the United States.

Mike's one-of-a-kind presentation style and his ability to simplify and clarify technical concepts explain his unique position as one of the premier educators and *Code* experts in the country. In addition to the materials he's produced, and the extensive list of companies around the world for whom he's provided training, Mike has written articles that have been seen in numerous industry magazines including, *Electrical Construction & Maintenance* (EC&M), *CEE News*, *Electrical Design and Installation* (EDI), *Electrical Contractor* (EC), *International Association of Electrical Inspectors* (IAEI News), *The Electrical Distributor* (TED), *Power Quality* (PQ), and *Solar Pro*.

Mike's ultimate goal has always been to increase electrical safety and improve lives and he is always looking for the best ways for his students to learn and teach the *Code* and pass electrical exams. His passion for the electrical field continues to grow and today he is more committed than ever to serve this industry.

His commitment to pushing boundaries and setting high standards extends into his personal life. Mike's an eight-time Overall National Barefoot Waterski Champion with more than 20 gold medals, and many national records, and he has competed in three World Barefoot Tournaments. In 2015, at the tender age of 64, he started a new adventure—competitive mountain bike racing. Every day he continues to find ways to motivate himself, both mentally and physically.

Mike and his wife, Linda, reside in New Mexico and Florida, and are the parents of seven children and six grandchildren. As his life has changed over the years, a few things have remained constant: his commitment to God, his love for his family, and doing what he can to change the lives of others through his products and seminars.

Special Acknowledgments

My Family. First, I want to thank God for my godly wife who's always by my side and also for my children.

My Staff. A personal thank you goes to my team at Mike Holt Enterprises for all the work they do to help me with my mission of changing peoples' lives through education. They work tirelessly to ensure that in addition to our products meeting and exceeding the educational needs of our customers, we stay committed to building life-long relationships with them throughout their electrical careers.

The National Fire Protection Association. A special thank you must be given to the staff at the National Fire Protection Association (NFPA), publishers of the *NEC*—in particular, Jeff Sargent for his assistance in answering my many *Code* questions over the years. Jeff, you're a "first class" guy, and I admire your dedication and commitment to helping others understand the *NEC*. Other former NFPA staff members I would like to thank include John Calogerro, Joe Ross, and Dick Murray for their help in the past.

PRACTICE EXAM INSTRUCTIONS

General

Obtaining an electrical license is a big step that will take your career to a whole new level. Proper preparation for your test is important to ensure your ultimate success. This practice exam is a diagnostic tool to help you evaluate your preparation for taking an exam, and is not a duplication of any actual licensing exam. You should use the results to evaluate the areas in which you need additional help to learn the material and prepare for your exam. This practice exam is comprised of three parts:

Part 1—*Electrical Theory* (4-Hour Limit)
Part 2—*National Electrical Code®* (4-Hour Limit)
Part 3—*Electrical Calculations* (6-Hour Limit)

Reference Books

To duplicate the test-taking experience, use the reference books you're permitted to bring into the testing room. You'll find the list of permitted reference materials in the Candidate Booklet provided by the state or the testing agency for your exam. If you are not permitted to use reference books other than the *NEC®*, you should take this test using only the *Code* book.

Materials

You'll need a blank sheet of paper, a calculator, approved reference books (see above), several pencils, and an alarm clock or timer.

Grading Your Practice Exam

Your score is important, but keep in mind that your goal in doing this practice exam is to determine your weakest areas so you know what you need to review. To grade your Answer Sheets, go to the corresponding Answer Key and grade each Part separately. Use the following formula:

Score (Number Correct Answers)/Total Number of Questions × 100 = Percentage Correct

Part 1 Score _____ / 100 × 100 = _____%

Part 2 Score _____ / 100 × 100 = _____%

Part 3 Score _____ / 60 × 100 = _____%

Reviewing Your Practice Exam

Once you have completed the practice exams, identify any areas of weakness by highlighting the questions you missed. This will help you identify areas you need to study to improve your score(s).

Any part of the exam on which you scored less than 75% is considered failing, and additional study is needed. If, after taking these exams you determine that you need additional help with your studies, *Mike Holt's Illustrated Guide to Electrical Exam Preparation*, *Illustrated Guide to Basic Electrical Theory*, and *Understanding the National Electrical Code* textbooks and videos can provide the training you need to pass the first time.

Passing Your Exam

Being prepared for an exam means more than just knowing electrical concepts, the *Code*, and calculations. Many good and knowledgeable electricians have not passed their exams because they did not know the proper way to get ready for an exam, or how to take a test. Preparing for your exam is a process. We encourage you to read the exam preparation tips in *Mike's Holt's Illustrated Guide to Electrical Exam Preparation* textbook, or visit www.MikeHolt.com/examtips for details on how to prepare for your exam, so that you are confident walking into the exam room.

Good luck and God bless!

Time Schedule | Practice Exam Instructions

Time Schedule

The total test time for these Practice Exams is 14 hours. We suggest that you complete each section on a different day. The following is a guide for how to schedule your practice exams. Adjust your start and finish times to allow the same amount of testing time as given in the following examples:

Part 1—Electrical Theory

7:55 a.m.: Go to Page 51 and tear out the Part 1—Electrical Theory Answer Sheet to record your answers. Set the alarm for 12:00 noon or set your timer for 4 hours (to mark the end of Part 1).

8:00 a.m.: Go to Page 1, start your timer, and begin Part 1—Electrical Theory Exam. Answer all questions as quickly and accurately as possible. If you finish early, do NOT start Part 2.

12:00 noon: Part 1 is over, even if you're not finished.

Part 2—National Electrical Code

7:55 a.m.: Go to Page 53 and tear out the Part 2—*National Electrical Code* Answer Sheet to record your answers. Set the alarm for 12:00 noon or set your timer for 4 hours (to mark the end of Part 2).

8:00 a.m.: Go to Page 11, start your timer, and begin Part 2—*National Electrical Code* Exam. Answer all questions as quickly and accurately as possible. If you finish early, do NOT start Part 3.

12:00 noon: Part 2 is over, even if you're not finished.

Part 3—Electrical Calculations

7:55 a.m.: Go to Page 55 and tear out the Part 3—Electrical Calculations Answer Sheet to record your answers. Set the alarm for 2:00 p.m. or set your timer for 6 hours (to mark the end of Part 3).

8:00 a.m.: Go to Page 21, start your timer, and begin Part 3—Electrical Calculations Exam. Use blank paper to work out the calculations.

2:00 p.m.: Part 3 is over, even if you're not finished.

Good luck!

PART 1

ELECTRICAL THEORY EXAM (4 HOURS)

The questions for this exam are extracted from *Mike Holt's Illustrated Guide to Basic Electrical Theory* textbook.

CHAPTER 1—ELECTRICAL FUNDAMENTALS

Unit 1—Matter

1. Providing a path to the earth often helps reduce electrostatic charge.

    (a) True
    (b) False

2. Lightning frequently terminates to a point of elevation and strikes nonmetallic as well as metallic objects with the same frequency.

    (a) True
    (b) False

3. The termination of the lightning stroke is unlikely to ignite combustible materials.

    (a) True
    (b) False

4. Lightning protection is intended to protect the building itself, as well as the electrical equipment on or inside the structure.

    (a) True
    (b) False

Unit 3—Magnetism

5. Nonmagnetic metals are ferrous, meaning they do not contain any iron, and cannot be magnetized.

    (a) True
    (b) False

6. Magnetic lines of force can cross each other and they are called flux lines.

    (a) True
    (b) False

Unit 4—Electricity

7. It is not the force of the magnetic field through a conductor that produces electricity; it is the relative motion of the field to the electrons within the conductor that produces the movement of electrons.

    (a) True
    (b) False

8. People become injured and death occurs when voltage pushes electrons through the human body causing the heart to go into ventricular fibrillation.

    (a) True
    (b) False

9. The severity of an electric shock is dependent on the current flowing through the body, which is impacted by circuit voltage and contact resistance.

    (a) True
    (b) False

Part 1 | Electrical Theory Exam

10. An electrical arc blast can approach _____, which vaporizes metal parts and produces an explosive and deadly pressure wave.
    - (a) 10,000°F
    - (b) 15,000°F
    - (c) 25,000°F
    - (d) 30,000°F

Unit 5—Electromagnetism

11. If a conductor carrying current is next to another conductor carrying current in the opposite direction, the electromagnetic field attempts to push the conductors apart.
    - (a) True
    - (b) False

Unit 6—Uses of Electromagnetism

12. A clamp-on ac ammeter has a coil that is clamped around the conductor and detects the rising and falling _____ field being produced due to the ac flow through the conductor.
    - (a) static
    - (b) current
    - (c) power
    - (d) magnetic

13. Ohmmeters measure the _____ or opposition to current flow of a circuit or component.
    - (a) voltage
    - (b) current
    - (c) power
    - (d) resistance

14. The megger is used to measure very high-_____ values, such as those found in cable insulation, or motor and transformer windings.
    - (a) voltage
    - (b) current
    - (c) power
    - (d) resistance

15. The electric motor works on the principle of the attracting and repelling forces of _____ fields.
    - (a) voltage
    - (b) current
    - (c) power
    - (d) magnetic

16. The _____ of a generator is forced to rotate while it is being subjected to the magnetic field of the stator.
    - (a) winding
    - (b) rotor
    - (c) stator
    - (d) b or c

17. A holding relay is primarily used for worker convenience.
    - (a) True
    - (b) False

CHAPTER 2—BASIC ELECTRICITY

Unit 7—The Electrical Circuit

18. According to the Electron Current Flow Theory, electrons flow away from the negative terminal of the source, through the circuit and load, toward the positive terminal of the source.
    - (a) True
    - (b) False

19. According to the Conventional Current Flow Theory, electrons travel from positive to negative.
    - (a) True
    - (b) False

Unit 9—Electrical Formulas

20. The major advantage of ac over dc is the ease of voltage regulation by the use of a transformer.
    - (a) True
    - (b) False

21. The best conductors, in order of their conductivity, are gold, silver, copper, and aluminum.
    - (a) True
    - (b) False

22. In a dc circuit, the only opposition to current flow is the physical resistance of the material. This opposition is called "reactance" and is measured in ohms.

    (a) True
    (b) False

23. What is the voltage drop of two 12 AWG conductors (0.40 ohms) supplying a 16A load, located 100 ft from the power supply? Formula: $E_{VD} = I \times R$

    (a) 1.60V
    (b) 3.20V
    (c) 6.40V
    (d) 12.80V

24. What is the resistance of the circuit conductors when the conductor voltage drop is 7.20V and the current flow is 50A?

    (a) 0.14 ohms
    (b) 0.30 ohms
    (c) 3 ohms
    (d) 14 ohms

25. What is the power loss in watts of a conductor that carries 24A and has a voltage drop of 7.20V?

    (a) 175W
    (b) 350W
    (c) 700W
    (d) 2,400W

26. What is the approximate power consumed by a 10 kW heat strip rated 230V, when connected to a 208V circuit?

    (a) 8 kW
    (b) 9 kW
    (c) 11 kW
    (d) 12 kW

27. The formulas in the formula wheel apply to _____.

    (a) dc
    (b) ac with unity power factor
    (c) dc or ac circuits
    (d) a and b

28. The total circuit resistance of two 12 AWG conductors (each 100 ft long) is 0.40 ohms. If the current of the circuit is 16A, what is the power loss of the conductors in watts?

    (a) 75W
    (b) 100W
    (c) 300W
    (d) 600W

29. What is the conductor power loss in watts for a 120V circuit that has a 3 percent voltage drop and carries a current flow of 12A?

    (a) 43W
    (b) 86W
    (c) 172W
    (d) 1,440W

30. What does it cost per year (at 8 cents per kWh) for the power loss of a 12 AWG circuit conductor (100 ft long) that has a total resistance of 0.40 ohm and current flow of 16A?

    (a) $30
    (b) $50
    (c) $70
    (d) $90

31. What is the power consumed by a 10 kW heat strip rated 230V connected to a 115V circuit?

    (a) 2.50 kW
    (b) 5 kW
    (c) 7.50 kW
    (d) 15 kW

CHAPTER 3—BASIC ELECTRICAL CIRCUITS

Unit 10—Series Circuits

32. The opposition to current flow results in voltage drop.

    (a) True
    (b) False

33. Kirchoff's Voltage Law states, "In a series circuit, the sum of the voltage drops across all of the resistors will equal the applied voltage."

    (a) True
    (b) False

34. Kirchoff's Current Law states, "In a series circuit, the current is _____ through the transformer, the conductors, and the appliance."

    (a) proportional
    (b) distributed
    (c) additive
    (d) the same

Unit 11—Parallel Circuits

35. According to Kirchoff's Current Law, the total current provided by the source to a parallel circuit will equal the sum of the currents of all of the branches.

    (a) True
    (b) False

36. The total resistance of a parallel circuit can be calculated by the _____ method.

    (a) equal resistance
    (b) product-over-sum
    (c) reciprocal
    (d) any of these

37. When power supplies are connected in parallel, the voltage remains the same, but the current or amp-hour capacity will be increased.

    (a) True
    (b) False

Unit 13—Multiwire Circuits

38. A balanced 3-wire, 120/240V, single-phase circuit is connected so that the ungrounded conductors are from different transformer phases (Line 1 and Line 2). The current on the neutral conductor will be _____ percent of the ungrounded conductor current.

    (a) 0
    (b) 70
    (c) 80
    (d) 100

39. If the ungrounded conductors of a multiwire circuit are not terminated to different phases, this can cause the neutral current to be in excess of the neutral conductor rating.

    (a) True
    (b) False

40. The current flowing on the neutral conductor of a multiwire circuit is called "unbalanced current."

    (a) True
    (b) False

41. Improper wiring or mishandling of multiwire branch circuits can cause _____ connected to the circuit.

    (a) overloading of the ungrounded conductors
    (b) overloading of the neutral conductors
    (c) destruction of equipment because of overvoltage
    (d) b and c

42. Because of the dangers associated with an open neutral conductor, the continuity of the _____ conductor cannot be dependent upon the receptacle.

    (a) ungrounded
    (b) grounded
    (c) a and b
    (d) none of these

CHAPTER 4—ELECTRICAL SYSTEMS AND PROTECTION

Unit 14—The Electrical System

43. Electrons leaving a power supply are always trying to return to the same power supply; they are not trying to go into the earth.

    (a) True
    (b) False

44. To prevent fires and electric shock, the NEC specifies that neutral current can flow on metal parts of the electrical system.

    (a) True
    (b) False

45. Metal parts of premises wiring must be bonded to a low-impedance path designed so that the circuit protection device will quickly open and clear a ground fault.

    (a) True
    (b) False

46. Because of the earth's _____ resistance to current flow, it cannot be used for the purpose of clearing a line-to-case ground fault.

    (a) low
    (b) high
    (c) variable
    (d) unpredictable

Unit 15—Protection Devices

Part A—Overcurrent Protection Devices

47. The purpose of overcurrent protection is to protect the conductors and equipment against excessive or dangerous temperatures because of overcurrent. Overcurrent is current in excess of the rated current of equipment or conductors. It may result from a(n) _____.

    (a) overload
    (b) short circuit
    (c) ground fault
    (d) all of these

48. To protect against electric shock or to prevent a fire, a dangerous _____ must quickly be removed by opening the circuit's overcurrent protection device.

    (a) overload
    (b) short circuit
    (c) ground fault
    (d) all of these

49. Inverse time breakers operate on the principle that as the current decreases, the time it takes for the device to open decreases.

    (a) True
    (b) False

50. The _____ sensing element causes the circuit breaker to open when a predetermined calibration temperature is reached.

    (a) magnetic
    (b) electronic
    (c) thermo
    (d) none of these

51. The magnetic time-delay circuit breaker operates on the solenoid principle where a movable core, held with a spring, is moved by the magnetic field of a(n) _____.

    (a) overload
    (b) short circuit
    (c) ground fault
    (d) b or c

52. Available short-circuit current is the current in amperes available at a given point in the electrical system.

    (a) True
    (b) False

53. Factors that affect the available short-circuit current include transformer _____.

    (a) voltage
    (b) kVA rating
    (c) impedance
    (d) all of these

54. Factors that affect the available short-circuit current include circuit conductor _____.

    (a) material
    (b) size
    (c) length
    (d) all of these

55. Circuit breakers and fuses are intended to interrupt the circuit, and they must have an ampere interrupting rating (AIR) sufficient for the available short-circuit current.

    (a) True
    (b) False

56. If the protection device is not rated to interrupt the current at the available fault values at its listed voltage rating, it can explode while attempting to clear the fault.

    (a) True
    (b) False

57. Equipment must have a(n) _____ current rating that permits the protection device to clear a short circuit or ground fault without extensive damage to the components of the circuit.

    (a) overload
    (b) short-circuit
    (c) ground-fault
    (d) b or c

Part 1 | Electrical Theory Exam

Part B—Ground-Fault Circuit Interrupters

58. A GFCI is designed to protect persons against electric shock. It operates on the principle of monitoring the imbalance of current between the circuit's _____ conductor.

    (a) ungrounded
    (b) grounded
    (c) equipment
    (d) a and b

59. A GFCI-protection device contains an internal monitor that prevents the device from being turned on if there is a neutral-to-case connection downstream of the device, but this only occurs if there is a load on the circuit.

    (a) True
    (b) False

60. Severe electric shock or death can occur if a person touches the ungrounded and the neutral conductors at the same time, even if the circuit is GFCI-protected.

    (a) True
    (b) False

61. Typically, when a GFCI-protection device fails, the switching contacts remain closed and the device will continue to provide power without GFCI protection.

    (a) True
    (b) False

Part C—Arc-Fault Circuit Interrupters

62. Arcing is defined as a luminous discharge of electricity across an insulating medium. Electric arcs operate at temperatures between _____ and expel small particles of very hot molten material.

    (a) 1,000 and 5,000°F
    (b) 2,000 and 10,000°F
    (c) 5,000 and 15,000°F
    (d) 10,000 and 25,000°F

63. Unsafe arcing faults can occur in one of two ways, as series arcing faults or as parallel arcing faults. The most dangerous is the parallel arcing fault.

    (a) True
    (b) False

64. An AFCI-protection device provides protection from an arcing fault by recognizing the characteristics unique to an arcing fault and by functioning to de-energize the circuit when an arc fault is detected.

    (a) True
    (b) False

CHAPTER 5—ALTERNATING CURRENT

Unit 16—Alternating Current

65. A nonsinusoidal waveform is created when _____ loads distort the voltage and current sine wave.

    (a) linear
    (b) resistive
    (c) inductive
    (d) nonlinear

66. When describing the relationship between voltage and current, the reference waveform is always _____.

    (a) current
    (b) resistance
    (c) voltage
    (d) none of these

67. The effective value is equal to the peak value _____.

    (a) times 0.707
    (b) times 1.41
    (c) times 2
    (d) times $\sqrt{3}$

Unit 17—Capacitance

68. Even when power is removed from the circuit, capacitors can store large amounts of energy for a long period of time. They can discharge and arc if inadvertently shorted or grounded out.

    (a) True
    (b) False

69. The opposition offered to the flow of ac current by a capacitor is called "capacitive reactance," which is expressed in ohms and abbreviated _____.

    (a) X_c
    (b) X_L
    (c) Z
    (d) none of these

Unit 18—Induction

70. The induced voltage in a conductor carrying alternating current opposes the change in current flowing through the conductor. The induced voltage that opposes the current flow is called "_____."

    (a) CEMF
    (b) counter-electromotive force
    (c) back-EMF
    (d) all of these

71. For ac circuits, the ac _____ of a conductor must be taken into consideration.

    (a) eddy currents
    (b) skin effect
    (c) resistance
    (d) all of these

72. The expanding and collapsing magnetic field within the conductor induces a voltage in the conductors (CEMF) that repels the flowing electrons toward the surface of the conductor. This is called "_____."

    (a) eddy currents
    (b) induced voltage
    (c) impedance
    (d) skin effect

73. The total opposition to current flow in ac circuits is called "_____" and measured in ohms.

    (a) resistance
    (b) reactance
    (c) impedance
    (d) skin effect

74. The abbreviation for impedance is _____.

    (a) X_L
    (b) X_C
    (c) Z
    (d) none of these

75. Self-induced voltage opposes the change in current flowing in the conductor. This is called "inductive reactance" and it is abbreviated _____.

    (a) X_L
    (b) X_C
    (c) Z
    (d) none of these

Unit 19—Power Factor and Efficiency

Part A—Power Factor

76. AC inductive or capacitive reactive loads cause the voltage and current to be in-phase with each other.

    (a) True
    (b) False

77. What size transformer is required for a 100A, 240V, single-phase noncontinuous load that has a power factor of 85 percent?

    (a) 15 kVA
    (b) 25 kVA
    (c) 37.50 kVA
    (d) 50 kVA

78. How many 20A, 120V circuits are required for forty-two, 300W luminaires (noncontinuous load) that have a power factor of 85 percent?

    (a) 4 circuits
    (b) 5 circuits
    (c) 7 circuits
    (d) 8 circuits

Part B—Efficiency

79. If the output is 1,600W and the equipment is 88 percent efficient, what are the input amperes at 120V?

    (a) 10A
    (b) 15A
    (c) 20A
    (d) 25A

CHAPTER 6—MOTORS, GENERATORS, AND TRANSFORMERS

Unit 20—Motors

Part A—Motor Basics

80. Dual-voltage ac motors are made with two field windings. The field windings are connected in _____ for low-voltage operation and in _____ for high-voltage operation.

    (a) series, parallel
    (b) parallel, series
    (c) series, series
    (d) parallel, parallel

Part 1 | Electrical Theory Exam

81. The motor FLA rating is used when sizing motor conductor size or circuit protection.

    (a) True
    (b) False

82. What is the nameplate FLA for a 20 hp, 208V, three-phase motor with 90 percent power factor and 80 percent efficiency?

    (a) 51A
    (b) 58A
    (c) 65A
    (d) 80A

83. When a motor starts, the current drawn is approximately _____ times the motor FLA; this is known as "motor locked-rotor amperes" (LRA).

    (a) 0.80
    (b) 1.25
    (c) 3
    (d) 6

84. If the rotating part of the motor winding is jammed so that it cannot rotate, no CEMF will be produced in the motor winding. Result—the motor operates at _____ and the windings will be destroyed by excessive heat.

    (a) FLA
    (b) FLC
    (c) LRC
    (d) any of these

Part C—Alternating-Current Motors

85. In an ac induction motor, the stator produces a rotating magnetic field that induces current in the rotor windings. The rotor current generates a magnetic field in opposition to the magnetic field of the stator, thereby causing the rotor to turn.

    (a) True
    (b) False

86. In a(n) _____ motor, the rotor is locked in step with the rotating stator field and is dragged along at the speed of the rotating magnetic field.

    (a) wound-rotor
    (b) induction
    (c) synchronous
    (d) squirrel-cage

87. _____ motors are fractional horsepower motors that operate equally well on ac and dc and are used for vacuum cleaners, electric drills, mixers, and light household appliances.

    (a) AC
    (b) Universal
    (c) Wound-rotor
    (d) Synchronous

88. Swapping _____ of the line conductors can reverse a three-phase ac motor's rotation.

    (a) one
    (b) two
    (c) three
    (d) four

Unit 21—Generators

89. The _____ of an ac generator contains the electromagnetic field, which cuts through the stationary conductor coils.

    (a) stator
    (b) rotor
    (c) coil
    (d) winding

90. Three-phase ac generators have three equally spaced windings, _____ degrees out-of-phase with each other.

    (a) 90
    (b) 120
    (c) 180
    (d) 360

Unit 22—Transformers

91. The energy transfer ability of a transformer is accomplished because the primary electromagnetic lines of force induce a voltage in the secondary winding.

    (a) True
    (b) False

92. Voltage induced in the secondary winding of a transformer is dependent on the number of secondary turns as compared to the number of primary turns.

    (a) True
    (b) False

93. Wasteful circulating _____ in the iron core cause(s) the core to heat up without any useful purpose.

    (a) conductor resistance
    (b) flux leakage
    (c) eddy currents
    (d) hysteresis losses

94. _____ can be reduced by dividing the core into many flat sections or laminations.

    (a) Conductor resistance
    (b) Flux leakage
    (c) Eddy currents
    (d) Hysteresis losses

95. As current flows through the transformer, the iron core is temporarily magnetized. The energy required to realign the core molecules to the changing electromagnetic field is called "_____" loss.

    (a) conductor resistance
    (b) flux leakage
    (c) eddy currents
    (d) hysteresis

96. Three-phase, _____, wye-connected systems can overheat because of circulating odd triplen harmonic currents.

    (a) 2-wire
    (b) 3-wire
    (c) 4-wire
    (d) none of these

97. The heating from harmonic currents is proportional to the square of the harmonic current.

    (a) True
    (b) False

98. Because of conductor resistance, flux leakage, eddy currents, and hysteresis losses, not all of the input power is transferred to the secondary winding for useful purposes.

    (a) True
    (b) False

99. If the primary phase voltage is 480V and the secondary phase voltage is 240V, the turns ratio is _____.

    (a) 1:2
    (b) 1:41
    (c) 2:1
    (d) 4:1

100. Transformers are rated in _____.

    (a) VA
    (b) kW
    (c) W
    (d) kVA

Suggested Study Materials:

Only when you truly know electrical theory can you have confidence in the practical aspects of your electrical work. **Mike Holt's Electrical Theory DVD Training Program** will give you the foundation you need to pass this portion of your exam. This program includes videos and *Mike Holt's Illustrated Guide to Basic Electrical Theory* textbook; it will help you understand what electricity is, how it's used and how it's produced. You'll learn everything from a brief study of matter to a breakdown of circuits for controls, fire alarms, security, and much more. You'll also learn the basics for motors and transformers. The full-color textbook provides hundreds of illustrated graphics, detailed examples, and practice questions to give you the training and practice you need to build your understanding of electrical theory.

Visit www.MikeHolt.com/Theory or call 888.632.2633.

Notes

PART 2

NATIONAL ELECTRICAL CODE EXAM (4 HOURS)

Please use the 2020 *Code* book to answer the following questions.

1. Overhead service-entrance cables shall be equipped with a _____.
   (a) raceway
   (b) service head
   (c) cover
   (d) all of these

2. Where portions of cable raceways or sleeves are required to be sealed due to different temperatures, sealants shall be identified for use with _____, a bare conductor, a shield, or other components.
   (a) low temperature conditions
   (b) high temperature conditions
   (c) a stranded conductor
   (d) the cable and conductor insulation

3. Grounding conductor connections to _____ for communications systems shall comply with 250.70.
   (a) ground rods
   (b) bonding jumpers
   (c) equipotential planes
   (d) grounding electrodes

4. A kit consisting of primary parts, which does not include all the parts for a complete subassembly but includes a list of required parts and installation instructions to complete the subassembly for a sign in the field is called a "_____ kit."
   (a) general use retrofit
   (b) reconditioning
   (c) maintenance
   (d) sign specific retrofit

5. For community antenna television and radio distribution communications systems, where the building or structure served has an intersystem bonding termination established, 250.94(A) shall apply.
   (a) True
   (b) False

6. The maximum number of disconnects for each PV system shall consist of not more than _____ switches or _____ sets of circuit breakers, or a combination of not more than _____ switches and sets of circuit breakers, mounted in a single enclosure, or in a group of separate enclosures.
   (a) one
   (b) six
   (c) eight
   (d) twelve

7. When a raceway is used for the support or protection of cables for fire alarm circuits, a bushing shall be installed where cables emerge from the raceway.
   (a) True
   (b) False

8. A dc circuit that is comprised of two monopole circuits, each having an opposite polarity connected to a common reference point is known as a "_____."
   (a) bipolar circuit
   (b) polar photovoltaic array
   (c) bipolar circuit or polar photovoltaic array
   (d) bidirectional circuit

Part 2 | National Electrical Code Exam

9. Unused openings for circuit breakers and switches in switchboards and panelboards shall be closed using _____, or other approved means that provide protection substantially equivalent to the wall of the enclosure.

   (a) duct seal and tape
   (b) identified closures
   (c) exothermic welding
   (d) sheet metal

10. One set of service-entrance conductors connected to the supply side of the normal service disconnecting means shall be permitted to supply standby power systems, fire pump equipment, and fire and sprinkler alarms covered by 230.82(5).

    (a) True
    (b) False

11. A(n) _____ conductor that carries only the unbalanced current from other conductors of the same circuit shall not be required to be counted when applying the provisions of 310.15(C)(1).

    (a) neutral
    (b) ungrounded
    (c) grounding
    (d) bonded

12. Where nonmetallic enclosures for switches are used with metal raceways or metal-armored cables, they shall comply with _____.

    (a) 314.12
    (b) 314.3 Ex 1
    (c) 314.3 Ex 2
    (d) 314.3 Ex 1 or 2

13. In bathrooms with less than the required zone required by 406.9(C), the receptacle(s) can be installed opposite the bathtub rim or shower stall threshold on the farthest wall within the room.

    (a) True
    (b) False

14. Luminaires and lighting equipment shall be connected to a(an) _____ conductor.

    (a) grounding electrode
    (b) grounded
    (c) equipment grounding
    (d) any of these

15. Receptacle outlets are required for kitchen countertops and work surfaces _____ in. and wider

    (a) 12
    (b) 15
    (c) 18
    (d) 24

16. Type NM cable and associated fittings shall be _____.

    (a) marked
    (b) approved
    (c) identified
    (d) listed

17. Compliance with the *Code* and proper maintenance result in an installation that is essentially _____.

    (a) free from hazards
    (b) not necessarily efficient or convenient
    (c) not necessarily adequate for good service or future expansion
    (d) all of these

18. Openings around penetrations of communications cables, communications raceways, and cable routing assemblies through fire-resistant-rated walls, partitions, floors, or ceilings shall be _____ using approved methods to maintain the fire resistance rating.

    (a) closed
    (b) opened
    (c) draft stopped
    (d) firestopped

19. Part I of Article 100 contains definitions intended to apply wherever the terms are used throughout this *Code*. Part III of Article 100 contains definitions for _____.

    (a) Hazardous (Classified) Locations
    (b) Solar (PV) Systems
    (c) Communications Systems
    (d) Grounding and Bonding

20. The requirement to run all paralleled circuit conductors within the same _____ applies separately to each portion of the paralleled installation.

    (a) raceway or auxiliary gutter
    (b) cable tray or trench
    (c) cable or cord
    (d) all of these

21. Running threads shall not be used on IMC for connection at couplings.

    (a) True
    (b) False

22. Class 1, Class 2, and Class 3 circuits installed _____ on the surface of ceilings and walls shall be supported by the building structure in such a manner that the cable will not be damaged by normal building use.

    (a) exposed
    (b) concealed
    (c) hidden
    (d) in raceways

23. Paint, plaster, cleaners, abrasives, corrosive residues, or other contaminants may result in an undetermined alteration of optical fiber cable _____.

    (a) usefulness
    (b) voltage
    (c) properties
    (d) reliability

24. Large-scale PV systems that do not provide arc-fault protection shall include details of fire mitigation plans to address _____ faults in the documentation required in 690.6.

    (a) dc arc
    (b) dc and ac arc
    (c) dc ground
    (d) dc and ac ground

25. Service-entrance and overhead service conductors shall be arranged so that _____ will not enter the service raceway or equipment.

    (a) dust
    (b) vapor
    (c) water
    (d) lightning

26. Electrical equipment and wiring methods in or on portable structures for carnival or circuses shall have mechanical protection where subject to _____.

    (a) public access
    (b) physical damage
    (c) exposure to the weather
    (d) operator access

27. For PV systems, the dc circuit conductors between modules and from modules to dc combiners, electronic power converters, or a dc PV system disconnecting means are known as the "PV _____ circuit."

    (a) source
    (b) array
    (c) input
    (d) output

28. All PV system circuit conductors, including the equipment grounding conductor, shall be _____ when they leave the vicinity of the PV array.

    (a) installed in the same raceway
    (b) installed in the same cable
    (c) run with PV array circuit conductors
    (d) any of these

29. In completed installations, each outlet box shall have a _____.

    (a) cover
    (b) faceplate
    (c) canopy
    (d) any of these

30. Where a branch circuit supplies continuous loads, or any combination of continuous and noncontinuous loads, the rating of the overcurrent device shall not be less than the noncontinuous load plus 125 percent of the continuous load.

    (a) True
    (b) False

31. Rigid metal conduit that is directly buried outdoors shall have at least _____ in. of cover.

    (a) 6
    (b) 12
    (c) 18
    (d) 24

32. Optical fiber cables not terminated at equipment other than a connector, and not identified for future use with a tag are considered abandoned.

    (a) True
    (b) False

33. Raceways permitted as a wiring method in Class II, Division 1 locations include _____.

    (a) threaded RMC and steel IMC
    (b) PVC conduit
    (c) electrical metallic tubing
    (d) any of these

34. Facilities with stand-alone systems shall have _____ installed in accordance with 710.10.

    (a) plaques
    (b) directories
    (c) plaques and directories
    (d) plaques or directories

35. Where used for emergency systems, the short-circuit current rating of the transfer equipment, based on the specific overcurrent protective device type and settings protecting the transfer equipment, shall be field marked on the _____ of the transfer equipment.

    (a) exterior
    (b) top
    (c) interior
    (d) underside

36. Openings around electrical penetrations into or through fire-resistant-rated walls, partitions, floors, or ceilings shall _____ to maintain the fire-resistance rating.

    (a) be documented
    (b) not be permitted
    (c) be firestopped using approved methods
    (d) be enlarged

37. Class 1, 2, and 3 circuits installed through fire-resistant-rated walls, partitions, floors, or ceilings shall be firestopped to limit the possible spread of fire or products of combustion.

    (a) True
    (b) False

38. For optional standby systems, the temporary connection of a portable generator without transfer equipment shall be permitted where conditions of maintenance and supervision ensure that only qualified persons will service the installation, and where the normal supply is physically isolated by _____.

    (a) a lockable disconnecting means
    (b) the disconnection of the normal supply conductors
    (c) an extended power outage
    (d) a lockable disconnecting means or the disconnection of the normal supply conductors

39. Audio system circuits using Class 2 or Class 3 wiring methods are not permitted in the same cable, raceway, or cable routing assembly with _____.

    (a) other audio system circuits
    (b) Class 1 conductors or cables
    (c) Class 3 conductors or cables
    (d) Class 2 conductors or Class 3 conductors or cables

40. A grounded conductor shall not be connected to normally noncurrent-carrying metal parts of equipment, to equipment grounding conductor(s), or be reconnected to ground on the load side of the _____ except as otherwise permitted.

    (a) service disconnecting means
    (b) distribution panel
    (c) switchgear
    (d) switchboard

41. In _____, type TC-ER-JP cable containing both power and control conductors shall be permitted for branch circuits and feeders.

    (a) multifamily dwellings
    (b) one- and two- family dwelling units
    (c) only duplexes
    (d) none of these

42. The construction and installation of electrical wiring for, and equipment in or adjacent to, all swimming, wading, therapeutic, and decorative pools is covered in Article _____.

    (a) 555
    (b) 600
    (c) 680
    (d) 690

43. The equipment grounding conductor at a marina is required to be an insulated conductor for all circuits.

    (a) True
    (b) False

44. Grounding electrodes of the rod type less than _____ in. in diameter shall be listed.

    (a) ½
    (b) ⅝
    (c) ¾
    (d) 1

45. As defined, the term "reconditioned" is frequently referred to as _____.

    (a) redeployed
    (b) redesigned
    (c) repurposed
    (d) refurbished

46. Receptacles shall be located not less than _____ ft from the inside walls of a storable pool, storable spa, or storable hot tub.

    (a) 5
    (b) 6
    (c) 15
    (d) 20

47. Cable trays shall be _____ except as permitted by 392.18(D).

    (a) exposed
    (b) accessible
    (c) readily accessible
    (d) exposed and accessible

48. All cut ends of LFMC conduit shall be _____ inside and outside to remove rough edges.

    (a) sanded
    (b) trimmed
    (c) brushed
    (d) any of these

49. The identification of terminals to which a neutral conductor is to be connected shall be substantially white or _____ in color.

    (a) clear
    (b) grey
    (c) silver
    (d) gold

50. Amplifiers, loudspeakers, and other equipment shall be located or protected so as to guard against environmental exposure or physical damage that might cause _____.

    (a) a fire
    (b) shock
    (c) personal hazard
    (d) all of these

51. Where radio or television equipment bonding or grounding is required, _____ used to connect a shield, a sheath, noncurrent-carrying metallic members of a cable, or metal parts of equipment or antennas to a bonding conductor or grounding electrode conductor shall be listed or be part of listed equipment.

    (a) fittings
    (b) clamps
    (c) lugs
    (d) devices

52. _____ drainage openings not smaller than ⅛ in. and not larger than ¼ in. in diameter shall be permitted to be installed in the field in boxes or conduit bodies listed for use in damp or wet locations.

    (a) Listed
    (b) Approved
    (c) Labeled
    (d) Identified

53. Permanent safety signs shall be installed to give notice of electrical shock hazard risks to persons using or swimming near a boat dock or marina and shall _____.

    (a) comply with 110.21(B)(1) and be of sufficient durability to withstand the environment
    (b) be clearly visible from all approaches to a marina, docking facility, or boatyard facility
    (c) state "WARNING—POTENTIAL SHOCK HAZARD—ELECTRICAL CURRENTS MAY BE PRESENT IN THE WATER."
    (d) all of these

54. Where rock bottom is encountered at an angle up to 45 degrees when driving a rod or pipe electrode, the electrode shall be permitted to be buried in a trench _____ deep.

    (a) 30 in.
    (b) 6 ft
    (c) 8 ft
    (d) 10 ft

55. The bonding jumper used to bond the metal water piping system shall be sized in accordance with _____ except as permitted in 250.104(A)(2) and 250.104(A)(3).

    (a) Table 250.102(C)(1)
    (b) Table 250.122
    (c) Table 310.16
    (d) Table 310.15(6)

56. All conductors of the same circuit shall be _____, unless otherwise specifically permitted in the *Code*.

    (a) bonded
    (b) grounded
    (c) the same size
    (d) in the same raceway or cable or be in close proximity in the same trench

57. Power-supply conductors and Class 1 circuit conductors can occupy the same cable, enclosure, or raceway without a barrier _____.

    (a) only where the equipment powered is functionally associated
    (b) where the circuits involved are not a mixture of ac and dc
    (c) under no circumstances
    (d) only where the equipment is essential for life safety

58. In accordance with Article 690, a "dc-to-dc _____ circuit" is the dc circuit conductors connected to the output of a dc combiner for dc-to-dc converter source circuits.

    (a) converter output
    (b) converter control
    (c) inverter output
    (d) inverter control

59. Each current-carrying conductor of a paralleled set of conductors shall be counted as a current-carrying conductor for the purpose of applying the adjustment factors of 310.15(C)(1).

    (a) True
    (b) False

60. In PV systems, where a single overcurrent device is used to protect a set of two or more parallel-connected module circuits, the ampacity of each of the module interconnection conductors shall not be less than the sum of the rating of the single overcurrent device plus _____ percent of the short-circuit current from the other parallel-connected modules.

    (a) 100
    (b) 115
    (c) 125
    (d) 150

61. In Class I locations, attachment plugs shall be of the type providing for _____ a permitted flexible cord and shall be identified for the location.

    (a) sealing compound around
    (b) quick connection to
    (c) connection to the equipment grounding conductor of
    (d) interlocking

62. Buildings whose sole purpose is to house and protect large-scale PV electric supply station equipment are required to include a rapid shutdown function to reduce shock hazard for firefighters.

    (a) True
    (b) False

63. The ampacity adjustment factors of 310.15(C)(1) shall not apply to conductors installed in surface metal raceways where the _____.

    (a) cross-sectional area exceeds 4 sq in.
    (b) current-carrying conductors do not exceed 30 in number
    (c) total cross-sectional area of all conductors does not exceed 20 percent of the interior cross-sectional area of the raceway
    (d) all of these

64. Conductors for general wiring not specifically permitted elsewhere in this *Code* to be covered or bare shall _____.

    (a) not be permitted
    (b) be insulated
    (c) be rated
    (d) be listed

65. Overcurrent devices for PV system dc circuits shall be rated to carry not less than _____ percent of the maximum currents calculated in 690.8(A).

    (a) 80
    (b) 100
    (c) 125
    (d) 250

66. In health care facilities, _____ ground receptacle(s) installed in patient care spaces outside of a patient care vicinity(s) shall comply with 517.16(B)(1) and (2).

    (a) AFCI-protected
    (b) GFCI-protected
    (c) isolated
    (d) all of these

67. In accordance with Article 690, a "functionally grounded system" has an electrical ground reference for operational purposes that is not _____ grounded.

    (a) effectively
    (b) sufficiently
    (c) solidly
    (d) any of these

68. An "appliance" is defined as utilization equipment, generally other than industrial, that is normally built in standardized sizes or types and is installed or connected as a unit to perform one or more functions such as clothes washing, air-conditioning, food mixing, deep frying and so forth.

    (a) True
    (b) False

69. The interconnected power production source conductors between power production equipment and the service or distribution equipment are known as the "_____."

    (a) power source input circuit
    (b) power source output circuit
    (c) input circuit conductors
    (d) output source conductors

70. A dwelling unit containing two 120V laundry branch circuits has a calculated load of _____ VA for the laundry circuits.

    (a) 1,500
    (b) 3,000
    (c) 4,500
    (d) 6,000

71. Fire alarm branch-circuit disconnecting means shall be permitted to be secured in the "on" position.

    (a) True
    (b) False

72. In Class I, Division 1 or Division 2 locations where the boxes, fittings, or enclosures are required to be explosionproof, if a flexible cord is used it shall terminate with a cord connector or attachment plug listed for the location, or a listed cord connector installed with a seal that is listed for the location. In Division 2 locations where explosionproof equipment is not required, the cord shall terminate _____.

    (a) with irreversible connections
    (b) with a listed receptacle
    (c) in a splice of any manner
    (d) with a listed cord connector or listed attachment plug

73. PV system dc circuit conductors shall be identified at all termination, connection, and splice points by separate color coding, marking tape, tagging, or other approved means.

    (a) True
    (b) False

74. Electrical connections in marinas, boatyards, and commercial and noncommercial docking facilities, shall be located _____ pier unless the conductor splices for floating piers are contained within sealed wire connector systems listed and identified for submersion.

    (a) at least 12 in. above the deck of a floating
    (b) at least 12 in. above the deck of a fixed
    (c) not below the electrical datum plane of a fixed
    (d) all of these

75. _____ may result in an undetermined alteration of communications wire and cable properties.

    (a) Paint or plaster
    (b) Cleaners or abrasives
    (c) Corrosive residues or other contaminants
    (d) any of these

76. All single-phase receptacles rated 150V to ground or less, 50A or less and three-phase receptacles rated 150V to ground or less, 100A or less installed in other than dwelling unit garages, service bays, and similar areas shall be GFCI protected, unless located in _____.

    (a) showrooms
    (b) vehicle exhibition halls
    (c) paint booths
    (d) showrooms and vehicle exhibition halls

77. The purpose of having all parallel conductor sets installed in metal wireways within the same group is to prevent _____ imbalance in the paralleled conductors due to inductive reactance.

    (a) current
    (b) voltage
    (c) inductive
    (d) all of these

78. The maximum PV inverter output circuit current is equal to the _____ output current rating.

    (a) average
    (b) peak
    (c) continuous
    (d) intermittent

79. Where a lighting outlet(s) is installed for interior stairways, there shall be a wall switch at each floor level and each landing level that includes an entryway where the stairway between floor levels has six risers or more unless remote, central, or automatic control is used.

    (a) True
    (b) False

80. Meter-mounted transfer switches shall be of the _____ type unless rated as determined by 702.4(B)(2).

    (a) automatic
    (b) manual
    (c) monitoring
    (d) remote

81. Where cables or nonmetallic raceways are installed through bored holes in joists, rafters, or wood members, holes shall be bored so that the edge of the hole is _____ the nearest edge of the wood member.

    (a) not less than 1¼ in. from
    (b) immediately adjacent to
    (c) not less than 1/16 in. from
    (d) 90 degrees away from

82. Metal faceplates for receptacles shall be grounded.

    (a) True
    (b) False

83. Underground raceways entering a(n) _____ from outside shall be sealed.

    (a) building or structure
    (b) crawlspace
    (c) highway right-of-way
    (d) easement

84. Threadless couplings approved for use with IMC in wet locations shall be _____.

    (a) rainproof
    (b) listed for wet locations
    (c) moistureproof
    (d) concrete-tight

85. Article 760 covers the requirements for the installation of wiring and equipment of _____.

    (a) communications systems
    (b) antennas
    (c) fire alarm systems
    (d) fiber optics

86. Optional standby system wiring is permitted to occupy the same raceways, cables, boxes, and cabinets with other general wiring.

    (a) True
    (b) False

87. Type NM cable can be installed as open runs in dropped or suspended ceilings in other than one- and two-family and multi-family dwellings.

    (a) True
    (b) False

88. The largest size grounding electrode conductor required is _____ copper.

    (a) 6 AWG
    (b) 1/0 AWG
    (c) 3/0 AWG
    (d) 250 kcmil

89. Where flexibility is required, which of the following wiring methods are permitted in a Class II, Division 1 location?

    (a) Dusttight flexible connectors.
    (b) Liquidtight flexible metal conduit with listed fittings.
    (c) Flexible cords listed for extra-hard usage with listed dusttight cord connectors.
    (d) any of these

90. The disconnecting means for air-conditioning and refrigerating equipment shall be _____ from the air-conditioning or refrigerating equipment.

    (a) accessible
    (b) located within sight
    (c) readily accessible
    (d) readily accessible from and located within sight

91. Where PV system disconnecting means of systems above _____ are readily accessible to unqualified persons, any enclosure door or hinged cover that exposes live parts when open shall be locked or require a tool to open.

    (a) 30V
    (b) 120V
    (c) 240V
    (d) 600V

92. Overhead feeder conductors shall have a minimum vertical clearance of _____ ft over residential property and driveways, as well as those commercial areas not subject to truck traffic, where the voltage does not exceed 300 volts-to-ground.

    (a) 10
    (b) 12
    (c) 15
    (d) 18

93. Where a luminaire stud or hickey is present in the box, _____ volume allowance in accordance with Table 314.16(B) shall be made for each type of fitting, based on the largest conductor present in the box.

    (a) a single
    (b) a double
    (c) a ¼
    (d) no additional

94. _____ shall be installed so that the wiring contained in them can be rendered accessible without removing any part of the building or structure or, in underground circuits, without excavating sidewalks, paving, or earth.

    (a) Boxes
    (b) Conduit bodies
    (c) Handhole enclosures
    (d) all of these

95. Any pit for which ventilation is not provided below a minor repair garage floor level of a lubrication or service room is considered to be a Class I, _____ location.

    (a) Division 1
    (b) Division 2
    (c) Division 1 or Division 2
    (d) Division 1 and Division 2

96. Accessible portions of abandoned fire alarm cable shall be removed.

    (a) True
    (b) False

97. A "dc-to-dc converter" is a device that can provide an output _____ voltage and current at a higher or lower value than the input _____ voltage and current.

    (a) ac, dc
    (b) ac, ac
    (c) dc, dc
    (d) dc, ac

98. The radius of the curve of the inner edge of any bend shall not be less than _____ for Type AC cable.

    (a) five times the largest conductor within the cable
    (b) three times the diameter of the cable
    (c) five times the diameter of the cable
    (d) six times the outside diameter of the conductors

99. When optical fiber cable is installed in a Chapter 3 raceway, the raceway shall be installed in accordance with Chapter 3 requirements.

    (a) True
    (b) False

100. Where the disconnecting means for a sign or outline lighting is not located within sight of the _____, a permanent field-applied marking identifying the location of the disconnecting means shall be applied to the controller in a location visible during servicing and the warning label shall comply with 110.21(B).

    (a) controller
    (b) branch circuit
    (c) feeder
    (d) photocell

Suggested Study Materials:

Knowing the *Code* and feeling confident in its application is the key to success on any electrical exam, and success in the field. **Mike's Understanding the *NEC* Complete Training Library** will give you the mastery you need to use your *Code* book successfully. This program is based on our bestselling *Understanding the National Electrical Code Volume 1 and 2* textbooks and videos, and also includes *Understanding NEC Requirements for Bonding and Grounding* textbook and *Understanding the National Electrical Code Workbook*. Topics include: General Requirements, Wiring and Protection, Grounding and Bonding, Wiring Methods and Materials, Equipment for General Use, Special Occupancies, Special Equipment, and Limited Energy and Communications Systems. Each book is filled with hundreds of detailed graphics and images to help you visualize the concepts clearly and to make it easy to understand the context. The videos follow the text as Mike and a panel of experts break down each article further to provide a deeper understanding of how they apply in the real world.

Invest in yourself, visit www.MikeHolt.com/Code to add this program to your own training library.

PART 3
ELECTRICAL CALCULATIONS EXAM (6 HOURS)

These questions relate directly to *Mike Holt's Illustrated Guide to Electrical Exam Preparation*, based on the 2020 NEC.

CHAPTER 1—ELECTRICAL FUNDAMENTALS

Unit 1—Basic Math, Advanced Math, and Electrical Circuits and Ohm's Law

1. What's the value of 160 increased by 75 percent?

    (a) 120
    (b) 280
    (c) 335
    (d) 28,000

2. $50{,}000W/(480V \times \sqrt{3})$ is equal to _____.

    (a) 60A
    (b) 100A
    (c) 200A
    (d) 480A

3. The product of 9, 18, 30, and 34 is equal to _____.

    (a) 100k
    (b) 125k
    (c) 150k
    (d) 165k

4. What's the surface area in sq ft of a two-story house that's 28 ft wide and 42 ft long?

    (a) 1,176 sq ft
    (b) 2,200 sq ft
    (c) 2,352 sq ft
    (d) 2,500 sq ft

5. What's the area of a raceway that has an inside diameter of 2½ in.?

    (a) 4.91 sq in.
    (b) 7.85 sq in.
    (c) 15.70 sq in.
    (d) 19.63 sq in.

6. If 240V supplies a resistive load of 112 ohms, what's the current flow in the circuit?

    (a) 2.14A
    (b) 10A
    (c) 12A
    (d) 20A

Unit 2—Electrical Circuits

7. What's the resistance total of a 10-ohm, a 6-ohm, and a 3-ohm resistor connected in parallel?

    (a) 0.60 ohms
    (b) 1.67 ohms
    (c) 19 ohms
    (d) 180 ohms

8. What's the voltage drop of 125 ft of 12 AWG wire (0.24 ohms) on a balanced 3-wire, 120/240V multiwire circuit supplying a 16A load?

    (a) 2.50V
    (b) 3.40V
    (c) 4.80V
    (d) 6.70V

Part 3 | Electrical Calculations Exam

Unit 3—Alternating Current

9. What's the current flow in amperes through a 1,800W load rated 120V when connected to a 120V power source?

    (a) 12A
    (b) 15A
    (c) 18A
    (d) 20A

10. What's the power loss of a 2-wire circuit carrying 12A having a length of 100 ft with two 12 AWG wires each having a resistance of 0.22 ohms?

    (a) 20W
    (b) 64W
    (c) 150W
    (d) 300W

11. What's the power loss for a 2-wire, 8 AWG circuit carrying 34A at 240V having a voltage drop of three percent?

    (a) 125W
    (b) 175W
    (c) 245W
    (d) 350W

12. What's the true power of a 24A load rated 120V with a power factor of 95 percent?

    (a) 1,632W
    (b) 1,800W
    (c) 1,920W
    (d) 2,736W

13. What's the apparent power in VA of a fluorescent ballast with a power factor of 90 percent when it's connected to two 40W bulbs?

    (a) 70 VA
    (b) 80 VA
    (c) 90 VA
    (d) 100 VA

14. What's the power factor for a ballast rated 0.50A at 277V supplying a 2 × 4 fixture containing four 32W bulbs?

    (a) 46%
    (b) 75%
    (c) 89%
    (d) 92%

15. What size kVA transformer is required for ninety-six, 150W electric discharge luminaires with a power factor of 95 percent?

    (a) 7.50 kVA
    (b) 10 kVA
    (c) 12.50 kVA
    (d) 15 kVA

16. If the output of a load is 3,282W and the equipment is 88 percent efficient, what's the input power rating in watts?

    (a) 2,000W
    (b) 2,500W
    (c) 3,285W
    (d) 3,730W

Unit 4—Motors and Transformers

17. What's the output watts of a 20 hp motor with an efficiency rating of 75 percent and a power factor of 70 percent?

    (a) 7.50 kW
    (b) 12.50 kW
    (c) 15 kW
    (d) 20 kW

18. What's the motor nameplate full-load amperes (FLA) for a 50 hp, 480V, three-phase motor having an efficiency rating of 80 percent and a power factor of 90 percent?

    (a) 70A
    (b) 84A
    (c) 99A
    (d) 115A

19. What's the secondary voltage of a transformer if the turns ratio is 4:1 and the primary voltage is 480V?

    (a) 60V
    (b) 120V
    (c) 240V
    (d) 480V

20. What's the turns ratio of a transformer if the primary phase voltage is 480V and the secondary is 208V?

    (a) 1:2
    (b) 2:1
    (c) 2.31:1
    (d) 4:1

CHAPTER 2—*NEC* CALCULATIONS

Unit 5—Raceway and Box Calculations

21. A trade size 3 Schedule 40 PVC raceway contains seven 1 RHW conductors without outer cover. How many 2 THW conductors may be installed in this raceway with the existing conductors?

    (a) 11 conductors
    (b) 15 conductors
    (c) 20 conductors
    (d) 25 conductors

22. What size wireway is required for three 400 kcmil THHN, one 250 kcmil THHN, four 4/0 THHN conductors, and three 8 THHN conductors?

    (a) 4 in. × 4 in. wireway
    (b) 6 in. × 6 in. wireway
    (c) 8 in. × 8 in. wireway
    (d) 10 in. × 10 in. wireway

23. Determine the minimum number of cubic inches required for two 10 AWG conductors passing through a box, four 14 AWG conductors spliced in the box, two 12 AWG conductors terminating to a receptacle, and one 12 AWG equipment bonding jumper from the receptacle to the box.

    (a) 15 cu in.
    (b) 20 cu in.
    (c) 21.75 cu in.
    (d) 22 cu in.

24. When determining the number of conductors in a box that has one 14/3 W/G NM cable, one switch, and two internal cable clamps, the count will equal _____.

    (a) 6 conductors
    (b) 7 conductors
    (c) 8 conductors
    (d) 10 conductors

▶Figure 1 applies to the next two questions.

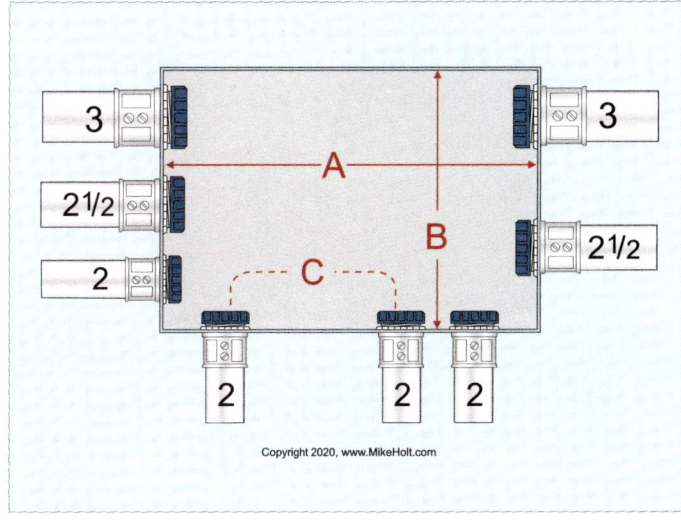

▶Figure 1

25. The minimum horizontal dimension for the junction box shown in the diagram in ▶Figure 1 is _____ in.

    (a) 18
    (b) 20
    (c) 21
    (d) 24

26. The minimum vertical dimension for the junction box shown in ▶Figure 1 is _____ in.

    (a) 16
    (b) 18
    (c) 20
    (d) 24

27. If a trade size 3 raceway entry (250 kcmil) is in the wall opposite a removable cover, the distance from that wall to the cover must not be less than _____ in.

    (a) 4
    (b) 4½
    (c) 5
    (d) 6

Part 3 | Electrical Calculations Exam

Unit 6—Conductor Sizing and Protection

28. What size THHN conductors are required to feed a 20A noncontinuous load when the conductors are in an ambient temperature of 120°F in a dry location? The circuit is protected with a 20A overcurrent device.

    (a) 14 AWG
    (b) 12 AWG
    (c) 10 AWG
    (d) 8 AWG

29. A(n) _____ THHN conductor is required for a 19.70A noncontinuous load if the ambient temperature is 75°F and there are nine current-carrying conductors in the raceway in a dry location.

    (a) 14
    (b) 12
    (c) 10
    (d) 8

30. The ampacity for each of nine current-carrying 10 THW conductors installed in a 20-in. long raceway is _____.

    (a) 25A
    (b) 30A
    (c) 35A
    (d) 40A

31. What's the ampacity of five 10 THWN-2 current-carrying conductors with an equipment grounding conductor in a PVC raceway located ½ in. above a roof, where the ambient temperature is 94°F?

    (a) 13.50A
    (b) 17.40A
    (c) 18.56A
    (d) 27.40A

32. A raceway contains the following: One 4-wire, multiwire branch circuit that supplies a balanced incandescent 120V lighting load; one 4-wire, multiwire branch circuit that supplies a balanced 120V fluorescent lighting load; two conductors that supply a receptacle; and one equipment grounding conductor. The system is 120/208V, three-phase. Taking these factors into consideration, how many of these conductors are considered current carrying?

    (a) 7 conductors
    (b) 8 conductors
    (c) 9 conductors
    (d) 11 conductors

33. There's a total of nine 10 THW conductors in a raceway. The system voltage is 120/208V, three-phase. One conductor is an equipment grounding conductor; four conductors supply a 4-wire, multiwire branch circuit for balanced electric-discharge luminaires; and the remaining conductors supply a 4-wire, multiwire branch circuit for balanced incandescent luminaires. Taking all these factors into consideration, how many of these conductors are considered current carrying?

    (a) 6 conductors
    (b) 7 conductors
    (c) 9 conductors
    (d) 10 conductors

34. What size overcurrent device is required for a 45A continuous load? The circuit is in a raceway with 14 current-carrying conductors.

    (a) 45A
    (b) 50A
    (c) 60A
    (d) 70A

35. A 1,200A feeder is tapped (over 10 ft but less than 25 ft long) to supply a 225A main breaker panelboard having a 180A continuous load. What's the minimum size THHN copper feeder tap conductor that can be used?

    (a) 1/0 AWG
    (b) 250 kcmil
    (c) 500 kcmil
    (d) 600 kcmil

Unit 7—Motor, Air-Conditioning, and Transformer Calculations

36. The branch-circuit conductors of a 5 hp, 230V, single-phase motor with a nameplate rating of 25A must have an ampacity of not less than _____.

    Note: This 5 hp motor is used for intermittent duty and, due to the nature of the apparatus it drives, it can't run for more than 5 minutes at any one time.

    (a) 22A
    (b) 23A
    (c) 33A
    (d) 37A

37. What size THHN feeder conductor is required for one 50 hp motor, one 20 hp motor, and two 10 hp motors where all of them are rated 480V, three-phase, with terminals rated 75°C?

    (a) 1/0 AWG
    (b) 2/0 AWG
    (c) 3/0 AWG
    (d) 4/0 AWG

38. The standard overload protective device for a 2 hp, 115V motor with a full-load current rating of 24A and a nameplate rating of 21.50A must not exceed _____.

    (a) 20.60A
    (b) 24.70A
    (c) 29.90A
    (d) 33.80A

39. The branch-circuit short-circuit and ground-fault protection (circuit breaker) for a 125 hp, 240V, direct-current motor is _____.

    (a) 400A
    (b) 600A
    (c) 700A
    (d) 800A

40. There are three motors; one 5 hp, 230V, single-phase motor with a service factor of 1.20; and two 1½ hp, 120V, single-phase motors. Using an inverse time breaker, the 3-wire feeder conductor protective device after balancing all three motors will be _____.

    (a) 60A
    (b) 70A
    (c) 80A
    (d) 90A

41. Which of the following statements about a 30 hp, 460V, three-phase synchronous motor and a 10 hp, 460V, three-phase motor is(are) true?

    (a) The 30 hp motor is supplied by 8 AWG conductors with an 80A breaker.
    (b) The 10 hp motor is supplied by 12 AWG conductors with a 35A breaker.
    (c) The feeder conductors must be 6 AWG with a 90A breaker.
    (d) all of these

42. What's the required feeder inverse time circuit breaker required for one 25 hp, 460V, three-phase squirrel-cage motor with a nameplate full-load current rating of 32A and a Design B service factor of 1.15; two 30 hp, 460V, three-phase wound-rotor motors with a nameplate primary full-load current rating of 38A and a nameplate secondary full-load current rating of 65A with a 40°C rise?

    (a) 150A
    (b) 175A
    (c) 200A
    (d) 225A

43. What's the VA load for the following five motors: 2 hp at 120V; 3 hp at 208V, single-phase; 5 hp at 208V, three-phase; 30 hp at 480V, three-phase; and 50 hp at 480V, three-phase?

    (a) 103,588 VA
    (b) 113,588 VA
    (c) 123,588 VA
    (d) 133,588 VA

44. The maximum size overcurrent device for primary only protection of a three-phase, 37.50 kVA, delta-delta configured transformer with a 480V primary and a 120/240V secondary is _____.

    (a) 40A
    (b) 45A
    (c) 50A
    (d) 60A

Unit 8—Voltage-Drop Calculations

45. A 240V, 40A, single-phase load is located 150 ft from an existing junction box. The junction box is located 50 ft from the panelboard and is wired with 4 AWG aluminum wire in a steel raceway. The total resistance of the two 4 AWG conductors from the panelboard to the junction box is approximately _____.

    (a) 0.03 ohms
    (b) 0.04 ohms
    (c) 0.05 ohms
    (d) 0.08 ohms

Part 3 | Electrical Calculations Exam

46. A load is located 100 ft from a 240V power supply and is wired with 4 AWG aluminum conductors. What size copper conductors can be used to replace the aluminum conductors without increasing the conductor voltage drop?

   (a) 8 AWG
   (b) 6 AWG
   (c) 2 AWG
   (d) 1/0 AWG

47. A 40A, 240V rated single-phase load is 150 ft from a junction box and the junction box is located 50 ft from a panelboard (for a total of 200 ft). If the voltage at the panelboard is 240V, what's the minimum voltage recommended by the NEC at the 40A load?

   (a) 117.70V
   (b) 228.20V
   (c) 232.80V
   (d) 236.20V

48. What's the voltage drop of two 3 AWG aluminum conductors that supply a 55A, 240V single-phase load? The motor is located 95 ft from the power supply.

   (a) 3.25V
   (b) 4.21V
   (c) 6.24V
   (d) 7.26V

49. How far can a 240V, 50A, three-phase load be located from a panelboard if it's fed with 3 AWG conductors and still meet the NEC recommendations for voltage drop for branch circuits?

   (a) 275 ft
   (b) 300 ft
   (c) 339 ft
   (d) 350 ft

50. Two 8 AWG copper conductors supply a 120V load that's located 225 ft from a panelboard. What's the maximum load in amperes that can be applied to these conductors without exceeding the NEC recommendation for conductor voltage drop?

   (a) 0A
   (b) 5A
   (c) 10A
   (d) 15A

Unit 9—Dwelling Unit Calculations

51. A 1,800 sq ft residence contains the following loads: One 1.50 kVA dishwasher, a 1 kVA disposal (waste), a pool motor (1.60 kVA), a 4 kW water heater, a 4.50 kW dryer, a 6 kW cooktop, two 3 kW ovens, a 28A, 240V air conditioner, and five 2 kW baseboard heaters. Using the optional method, the service size will be _____ for a 120/240V single-phase system with terminals rated 75°C.

   (a) 100A
   (b) 110A
   (c) 125A
   (d) 150A

52. Using the optional load calculations, what's the service demand load for an air conditioner/heat pump (20A at 240V) and five separate space-electric heating units at 2 kW each for a dwelling unit?

   (a) 4,280 VA
   (b) 4,800 VA
   (c) 4,875 VA
   (d) 9,675 VA

53. Using the optional method, calculate the service load in amperes for a 2,200 sq ft single-family dwelling containing the following loads: dishwasher 1.20 kVA at 120V, disposal (waste) 8A at 120V, water heater 4.50 kW, attic fan 16A at 120V, dryer 5 kW at 240V, range 14 kW at 240V, two air-conditioning units 10A at 240V, and electric heat 6 kW at 240V.

   (a) 98A
   (b) 109A
   (c) 121A
   (d) 130A

54. A dwelling unit contains a 5.50 kW electric clothes dryer. What's the feeder demand load for the dryer?

   (a) 3.38 kW
   (b) 4.50 kW
   (c) 5 kW
   (d) 5.50 kW

55. A dwelling unit has one 6 kW cooktop and one 6 kW oven. What's the minimum feeder demand load for the cooking appliances?

   (a) 6.50 kW
   (b) 7.10 kW
   (c) 7.80 kW
   (d) 8.20 kW

56. The minimum feeder demand load for two 3 kW wall-mounted ovens and one 6 kW cooktop is _____.

    (a) 8.40 kW
    (b) 9.30 kW
    (c) 9.60 kW
    (d) 11 kW

57. What's the service demand load for two 6 kW ovens, one 3.50 kW cooktop, and three 8 kW ranges?

    (a) 9 kW
    (b) 11 kW
    (c) 13 kW
    (d) 17 kW

58. What's the branch-circuit demand load for two 3 kW ovens and one 6 kW cooktop in a dwelling unit?

    (a) 4.50 kW
    (b) 4.80 kW
    (c) 6 kW
    (d) 8 kW

59. Using the standard method, calculate the service demand load in amperes for a 2,200 sq ft single-family dwelling containing the following loads: range 14.40 kW at 240, dryer 4.80 kW at 240V, dishwasher 1.20 kVA at 120V, disposal (waste) 9.80A at 120V, water heater 4.20 kW, two air-conditioning units 12A at 120V, and electric heat 6 kW at 240V.

    (a) 122A
    (b) 133A
    (c) 146A
    (d) 153A

60. Using the standard method, calculate the service neutral load for a 950 sq ft single-family dwelling containing the following loads: range 8 kW at 240V, dryer 4.50 kW at 240V, dishwasher 12A at 120V, water heater 4 kW at 240V, air conditioner 28A at 240V, and electric heat 9.60 kW at 240V.

    (a) 58A
    (b) 62A
    (c) 79A
    (d) 87A

Suggested Study Materials:

If you only need help with Calculations or you need additional training on Theory and *Code* as well, Mike provides many options for Exam Prep training. Whether you choose one of his in-depth libraries that provides a full study program for Theory, *Code* and Calculations, or you choose one of his streamlined fast track libraries, you'll find a program that works for you. All programs provide colorful fully illustrated textbooks, and informative videos that can help you pass your exam the first time. Choose the program that best fits your needs and find out why, for over 40 years, his study programs have successfully helped thousands of people pass their exams.

For more information, contact our office at 888.632.2633 and we can help you select study materials that fit your needs or visit www.MikeHolt.com/ExamPrep for additional information. Give yourself the tools you need to walk into any electrical exam with confidence; choose a Mike Holt training library today.

Notes

PART 1
ELECTRICAL THEORY ANSWER KEY

1. (a) True
2. (a) True
3. (b) False
4. (b) False
5. (b) False
6. (b) False
7. (a) True
8. (a) True
9. (a) True
10. (d) 30,000°F
11. (a) True
12. (d) magnetic
13. (d) resistance
14. (d) resistance
15. (d) magnetic
16. (b) rotor
17. (b) False
18. (a) True
19. (a) True
20. (a) True
21. (b) False
22. (b) False
23. (c) 6.40V

    EVD = I × R

    EVD = 16A × 0.40Ω

    EVD = 6.40V

24. (a) 0.14 ohms

    R = E/I

    R = 7.20V/50A

    R = 0.14 ohms

25. (a) 175W

    P = I × E

    P = 24A × 7.20V

    P = 172.80W

26. (a) 8 kW

    The power of the heat strip will be less because the applied voltage (208V) is less than the equipment voltage rating (230V). To calculate this, we must determine the heat strip resistance rating at 230V, and then determine the power rating at 208V based on the heat strip resistance rating.

    P = E²/R

    E = Applied Voltage = 208V

    R = Resistance of Heat Strip = E2/P

    Heat Strip Voltage Rating = 230V

    Power Rating of Heat Strip = 10,000W

    Resistance of Heat Strip = 230V2/10,000W

    Resistance of Heat Strip = 5.29Ω

    P = E²/R

    P = (208V × 208V)/5.29Ω

    P = 43,624/5.29Ω

    P = 8,178W/1,000

    P = 8.20 kW

27. (d) a and b
28. (b) 100W

    P = I² × R

    I = 16A

    R = 0.40Ω

    P = (16A × 16A) × 0.40Ω

    P = 102.40W

29. (a) 43W

    P = I × E

    I = 12A

    E = 120V × 3%

    E = 3.60V

    P = 12A × 3.60V

    P = 43.20W

Part 1 | Electrical Theory Answer Key

30. (c) $70

    Cost per Year = Power for the Year in kWh × $0.08
    Power per Hour = $I^2 \times R$
    I = 16A
    R = 0.40Ω
    Power per Hour = (16A × 16A) × 0.40Ω
    Power per Hour = 102.40W
    Power for the Year in kWh = (102.40W × 24 hours × 365 days)/1,000
    Power for the Year in kWh = 897 kWh
    Cost per Year = 897 kWh × $0.08
    Cost per Year = $71.76

31. (a) 2.50 kW

    The power of the heat strip will be less because the applied voltage (115V) is less than the equipment voltage rating (230V). To calculate this, we must determine the heat strip resistance rating at 230V, and then determine the power rating at 115V based on the heat strip resistance rating.
    $P = E^2/R$
    E = Applied Voltage = 115V
    R = Resistance of Heat Strip = E^2/P
    Heat Strip Voltage Rating = 230V
    Power Rating of Heat Strip = 10,000W
    Resistance of Heat Strip = $230V^2/10{,}000W$
    Resistance of Heat Strip = 5.29Ω
    $P = E^2/R$
    P = 13,225/5.29Ω
    P = 2,500W/1,000 = 2.50 kW
    Note: Power changes with the square of the voltage. If the voltage is reduced to 50%, then the power consumed will be equal to the new voltage percent^2 or 50%^{2}, or 10,000 × (0.50 × 0.50 = 0.25 = 25%) = 2,500W.

32. (a) True
33. (a) True
34. (d) the same
35. (a) True
36. (d) any of these
37. (a) True
38. (a) 0
39. (a) True
40. (a) True
41. (d) b and c
42. (b) grounded
43. (a) True
44. (b) False
45. (a) True
46. (b) high
47. (d) all of these
48. (d) all of these
49. (b) False
50. (c) thermo
51. (d) b or c
52. (a) True
53. (d) all of these
54. (d) all of these
55. (a) True
56. (a) True
57. (b) short-circuit
58. (d) a and b
59. (b) False
60. (a) True
61. (a) True
62. (c) 5,000 and 15,000°F
63. (a) True
64. (a) True
65. (d) nonlinear
66. (c) voltage
67. (a) times 0.707
68. (a) True
69. (a) X_C
70. (d) all of these
71. (d) all of these
72. (d) skin effect
73. (c) impedance
74. (c) Z
75. (a) X_L
76. (b) False
77. (b) 25 kVA

    Load kVA = (Volts × Amperes)/1,000
    Load kVA = (240V × 100A)/1,000
    Load kVA = 24 kVA
    Note: If a question gives you the current, voltage, and power factor, and asks for the VA load, then simply multiply the Volts given by the Amperes given; ignore the Power Factor distractor in the question.

78. (c) 7 circuits

   VA per Circuit = Volts × Amperes

   VA per Circuit = 120V × 20A

   VA per Circuit = 2,400 VA

   VA per Luminaire = Watts/Power Factor

   VA per Luminaire = 300W/0.85 PF

   VA per Luminaire = 353 VA

   Lights per Circuit = 2,400 VA/353 VA = 6.80

   Lights per Circuit = 6

   Circuits = 42 luminaires/6 per circuit

   Circuits = 7

79. (b) 15A

   Input = Output/Efficiency

   Input = 1,600W/0.88 Eff

   Input = 1,818W

   Input Amperes = Watts/Volts

   Input Amperes = 1,818W/120V

   Input Amperes = 15.167A

80. (b) parallel, series
81. (b) False
82. (b) 58A

   FLA = (hp × 746W)/(V × 1.732 × PF × Eff)

   FLA = (20 hp × 746W)/(208V × 1.732 × 0.90 PF × 0.80 Eff)

   FLA = 58A

83. (d) 6
84. (c) LRC
85. (a) True
86. (c) synchronous
87. (b) Universal
88. (b) two
89. (b) rotor
90. (b) 120
91. (a) True
92. (a) True
93. (c) eddy currents
94. (c) Eddy currents
95. (d) hysteresis
96. (c) 4-wire
97. (a) True
98. (a) True
99. (c) 2:1
100. (d) kVA

Notes

PART 2

NATIONAL ELECTRICAL CODE ANSWER KEY

Question	Answer	NEC Section
1.	(b)	230.54(B)
2.	(d)	300.7(A)
3.	(d)	800.100(C)
4.	(a)	600.2 Retrofit Kit, General Use
5.	(a)	800.100(B)(2)
6.	(b)	690.13(C)
7.	(a)	760.3(K) and 300.15(C)
8.	(a)	690.2 Bipolar Circuit
9.	(b)	408.7
10.	(a)	230.40 Ex 5
11.	(a)	310.15(E)(1)
12.	(d)	404.12
13.	(a)	406.9(C) Ex
14.	(c)	410.40
15.	(a)	210.52(C)
16.	(d)	334.6
17.	(d)	90.1(B)
18.	(d)	800.26
19.	(a)	100 Scope
20.	(d)	300.3(B)(1)
21.	(a)	342.42(B)
22.	(a)	725.24
23.	(c)	770.24 Note 3
24.	(a)	691.10
25.	(c)	230.54(G)
26.	(b)	525.6
27.	(a)	690.2 PV Source Circuit
28.	(d)	690.43(C)
29.	(d)	314.25
30.	(a)	210.20(A)
31.	(a)	300.5(A) and Table 300.5 Column 2
32.	(a)	770.2 Abandoned Optical Fiber Cable
33.	(a)	502.10(A)(1)(1)
34.	(d)	690.56(A)
35.	(a)	700.5(E)
36.	(c)	300.21
37.	(a)	725.3(B) and 300.21
38.	(d)	702.5(A) Ex
39.	(d)	725.139(F)
40.	(a)	250.24(A)(5)
41.	(b)	336.10(9)
42.	(c)	680.1
43.	(a)	555.37(B)
44.	(b)	250.52(A)(5)(b)
45.	(d)	100 Reconditioned, Note
46.	(b)	680.34
47.	(d)	392.18(E)
48.	(b)	350.28
49.	(c)	200.9
50.	(d)	640.4
51.	(d)	810.7
52.	(b)	314.15
53.	(d)	555.10(1), (2), and (3)
54.	(a)	250.53(A)(4)
55.	(a)	250.104(A)(1)
56.	(d)	300.5(I) and 300.3(B)
57.	(a)	725.48(B)(1)
58.	(a)	690.2 DC-to-DC Converter Output Circuit
59.	(a)	310.15(C)(1)
60.	(c)	690.8(D)
61.	(c)	501.145(B)
62.	(b)	691.9
63.	(d)	386.22(1), (2), and (3)
64.	(b)	310.3(D)
65.	(c)	690.9(B)(1)
66.	(c)	517.16(B)
67.	(c)	690.2 Grounded (Functionally)
68.	(a)	100 Appliance
69.	(b)	705.2 Power Source Output Circuit
70.	(b)	220.52(B)
71.	(a)	760.121(B)
72.	(d)	501.140(B)(4)
73.	(a)	690.31(B)(1)
74.	(d)	555.30(A) and (B)

Part 2 | National Electrical Code Answer Key

Question	Answer	NEC Section
75.	(d)	800.24 Note 3
76.	(d)	210.8(B)(8)
77.	(a)	376.20 Note
78.	(c)	690.8(A)(1)(c)
79.	(a)	210.70(A)(2)(3)
80.	(b)	702.5(B)
81.	(a)	300.4(A)(1)
82.	(a)	406.6(B)
83.	(a)	225.27
84.	(b)	342.42(A)
85.	(c)	760.1
86.	(a)	702.10
87.	(b)	334.12(A)(2)

Question	Answer	NEC Section
88.	(c)	250.66 and Table 250.66
89.	(d)	502.10(A)(2)(1), (2), and (5)
90.	(d)	440.14
91.	(a)	690.13(A)
92.	(b)	225.18(2)
93.	(a)	314.16(B)(3)
94.	(d)	314.29(A) and (B)
95.	(b)	511.3(C) and Table 511.3(C)
96.	(a)	760.25
97.	(c)	100 DC-to-DC Converter
98.	(c)	320.24
99.	(a)	770.110(A)(1)
100.	(a)	600.6(A)(3) Ex

PART 3

ELECTRICAL CALCULATIONS ANSWER KEY

Note: The calculations are shown immediately following the answers. Methods other than the ones we used may be correct in some cases. If you used a different method of calculation to come up with the same answer, it's probably okay.

CHAPTER 1—ELECTRICAL FUNDAMENTALS

Unit 1—Basic Math, Advanced Math, and Electrical Circuits and Ohm's Law

1. **(b) 280**

    Step 1: Convert 75 percent to decimal form: 0.75
    Step 2: Add one to the decimal value: 1 +0.75 = 1.75
    Step 3: Multiply 160 (the original number) by the multiplier of 1.75: 160 × 1.75 = 280.

2. **(a) 60A**

    Step 1: Determine the decimal value for the $\sqrt{3}$ = 1.732.
    Step 2: Divide 50,000W by (480V × 1.732).

    50,000W/(480V × 1.732)
    50,000W/861.36V = 100A
    1.11 Kilo

3. **(d) 165k**

    9 × 18 × 30 × 34 = 165,240
    165.240/1,000 = 165.240k

4. **(c) 2,352 sq ft**

    Area = L × W × 2 (number of floors)
    Area = 42 ft × 28 ft × 2
    Area = 2,352 sq ft

5. **(a) 4.91 sq in.**

    Area = $\pi \times r^2$
    π is equal to 3.14.
    Radius (r) is equal to the diameter by 0.50.
    Area = 3.14 × (2.5 × 0.50)^2
    Area = 3.14 × (1.25)^2
    Area = 3.14 × (1.25 × 1.25)
    Area = 3.14 × 1.5625
    Area = 4.906 sq in.

    When using your calculator, follow these steps:

    Step 1: Find the radius by multiplying 0.50 by 2.5.
    Radius = 2.5 × 0.50
    Radius = 1.25
    Step 1: Press the square "×^{2}" key: 1.5625
    Step 3: Multiply 1.5625 by 3.14.
    1.5625 × 3.14 = 4.90625 sq in. (round to 4.91)

6. **(a) 2.14A**

    Step 1: What's the question? What is "I"?
    Step 2: What do you know? E = 240V and R = 112 ohms.
    Step 3: The formula to use is **I = E/R**.
    Step 4: The answer is I = 240V/112 ohms.
    Step 5: The answer is I = 2.14A.

Unit 2—Electrical Circuits

7. **(b) 1.67 ohms**

    Use your calculator for this problem.

    Step 1: Add the reciprocals of all the resistors together.
    Step 2: Calculate the total resistance using the formula:
    $R_T = 1/(1/R_1 +1/R_2 +1/R_3)$
    $R_T = 1/(1/10 + 1/6 + 1/3)$
    $R_T = 1/(10 \text{ [press "1/x"]} +6 \text{ [press "1/x"]} + 3 \text{ [press "1/x"]})$
    R_T = (0.6 ohms) [press "1/x"]
    R_T = 1.666 ohms; round up to 1.67 ohms

Part 3 | Electrical Calculations Answer Key

8. (d) 6.70V

    $E_{VD} = I \times R$
    I = 16A
    R = (1.93 ohms per 1,000 ft/1,000) × 125 ft × 1 wire
    R = 0.24 ohms
    E_{VD} = 16A × 0.24 ohms
    E_{VD} = 6.70V dropped on phase wire

Unit 3—Alternating Current

9. (b) 15A

    Step 1: What is the question? What's "I"?
    Step 2: What do you know?
    Power Rating, P = 1800W
    Voltage Rating, E = 120V
    Step 3: The formula is **I = P/E**.
    Step 4: The answer is I = 1,800/120V.
    Step 5: The answer is 15A.

10. (b) 64W

    Step 1: What's the question? What's the power loss of the wires in watts? "P."
    Step 2: What do you know about the circuit?
    I = 12A
    R = 0.22 ohms per wire × 2 wires
    R = 0.44 ohms
    Step 3: What's the formula? **P = I² × R**
    Step 4: Calculate the answer:
    P = 12A² × 0.44 ohms
    P = (12A × 12A) × 0.44 ohms
    P = 144A × 0.44 ohms
    P = 63.36W (round up 64W)

11. (c) 245W

    Step 1: What's the question asking you to find? What's wasted? "P."
    Step 2: What do you know about the wires?
    I = 34A
    E_{VD} = 240V × 3%
    E_{VD} = 7.20 VD
    Step 3: The formula is **P = I × E**.
    Step 4: Calculate the answer:
    P = 34A × 7.20V
    P = 244.8W

12. (d) 2,736W

    True Power (P) in Watts =
    Apparent Power (VA) × Power Factor (PF)
    VA = E × I
    VA = 120V × 24A
    VA = 2,880 VA
    Watts = 2,880 VA × 0.95 PF
    Watts = 2,736W

13. (c) 90 VA

    Apparent Power (VA) = True Power (P) in Watts/Power Factor (PF)
    VA = P/PF
    VA = 80W/0.9 PF
    VA = 88.89 VA

    Apparent power is expressed in VA; therefore, neither (a) nor (d) can be the correct answer.

14. (d) 92%

    Power Factor (PF) =
    True Power (P) in Watts/Apparent Power (VA)
    PF = P/VA
    P = 32W × 4 bulbs
    P = 128W
    VA = Rated "I" of ballast × rated "E" of ballast
    VA = 0.50A × 277V
    VA = 139 VA
    PF = 128W/139 VA
    PF = 0.920 or 92%

15. (d) 15 kVA

    kW = (96 luminaires × 150W)/1,000
    kW = 14,400W/1,000
    kW = 14.4 kW
    Apparent Power = kW/PF
    Apparent Power = 14.4 kW/95% PF
    Apparent Power = 13.68 kVA

16. (d) 3,730W

    Input is always greater than the output.
    Input = Output Watts/Efficiency
    Input = 3,282W/88% Efficiency
    Input = 284W

Unit 4—Motors and Transformers

17. (c) 15 kW

   Output watts are based on horsepower only. Efficiency and power factor impacts the input power, not the output power.

   Output Watts = hp × 746W
   Output Watts = 20 hp × 746W
   Output Watts = 14,920W
   Output Watts = 14,920W/1,000
   Output Watts = 14.92 kW

18. (a) 70A

   FLA = (hp × 746W)/(E × 1.732 × Eff × PF)
   FLA = (50 hp × 746W)/(480V × 1.732 × 0.80 Eff × 0.90 PF)
   FLA = (62.31) 70A
   OR

   Step 1: Determine the motor output watts.
   Output Watts = hp × 746W
   Output Watts = 50 hp × 746W
   Output Watts = 37,300W

   Step 2: Determine the motor input watts.
   Input Watts = Output/Eff
   Input Watts = 37,300W/0.80 Eff
   Input Watts = 46,625W

   Step 3: Determine the motor input VA.
   VA = Watts/PF
   VA = 46,625W/0.90 PF
   VA = 51,806 VA

   Step 4: Determine the motor amperes.
   FLA = VA/(E × 1.732)
   FLA = 51,806 VA/(480V × 1.732)
   FLA = (62.31) 70A

19. (b) 120V

   Turns Ratio = Primary : Secondary
   Since the primary voltage is 240V, the secondary voltage is 10 times smaller: 480V/4 = 120V

20. (c) 2.31:1

   Turns Ratio = Primary : Secondary
   Step 1: E_P = 480V, E_S = 208V
   Step 2: Find ratio = 480V / 208V
   Step 3: Ratio = 2.31:1

Part 3 | Electrical Calculations Answer Key

CHAPTER 2—*NEC* CALCULATIONS

Unit 5—Raceway and Box Calculations

21. (a) 11 conductors

   Area conductor fill for a trade size 3, Schedule 40 PVC (RNC) raceway: 2.907 sq in., Chapter 9, Table 4, 40% column
   Area 1 RHW without cover: 0.1901 sq in., Chapter 9, Table 5

   Area of Seven 1 RHW Conductors = 0.1901 × 7 conductors
   Area of Seven 1 RHW Conductors = 1.3307 sq in.

   Spare Space = 2.907 sq in. - 1.3307 sq in.
   Spare Space = 1.5763 sq in.

   Quantity of 2 THW Permitted in Spare Space = 1.5763 sq in./0.1333
   Quantity of 2 THW Permitted in Spare Space = 11.80 conductors

   Note: The answer is 11 conductors. We only round up to the next size when all of the conductors are the same size (total cross-sectional area including insulation) and the calculation results in a decimal of 0.80 or greater. See Chapter 9, Table 1, Note 7.

22. (b) 6 in. × 6 in. wireway

   Conductor area, Chapter 9, Table 5:

400 kcmil THHN	0.5863 sq in. × 3 conductors	1.7589 sq in.
250 kcmil THHN	0.3970 sq in. × 1 conductor	0.3970 sq in.
4/0 THHN	0.3237 × 4 conductors	1.2948 sq in.
8 THHN	0.0366 × 3 conductors	+0.1098 sq in.
Total Conductor Area		3.5605 sq in.

   The wireway must not be filled over 20%, 376.22(A).

   Minimum Wireway = 3.5607/20%
   Minimum Wireway = 17.80 sq in.

   A 4 in. × 4 in. wireway has a cross-sectional area of 16 sq in. and is too small.
   A 6 in. × 6 in. wireway has a cross-sectional area of 36 sq in. and will be large enough.

23. (d) 22 cu in.

2—10 AWG passing through	2—10 AWG
1—1 yoke (receptacle)	2—12 AWG
4—14 AWG spliced in the box	4—14 AWG
2—12 AWG for terminating	2—12 AWG
1—12 AWG bonding jumper	0—12 AWG

   Total: Two 10 AWG conductors, four 12 AWG conductors, and four 14 AWG conductors.

   Note: insulation type doesn't matter for box fill calculations.

   Volume of the conductors, Table 314.16(B)

10 AWG: 2.50 cu in. × 2 conductors	5 cu in.
12 AWG: 2.25 cu in. × 4 conductors	9 cu in.
14 AWG: 2 cu in. × 4 conductors	+8 cu in.
Total	22 cu in.

24. (b) 7 conductors

   314.16(B)

   Volume of the conductors:

1—14/3	3—14 AWG conductors
1—Ground	1—14 AWG conductor
1—switch	2—14 AWG conductors
2—clamps	1—14 AWG conductor
Total Count	7—14 AWG conductors

▶Figure 1 applies to answers 25 and 26.

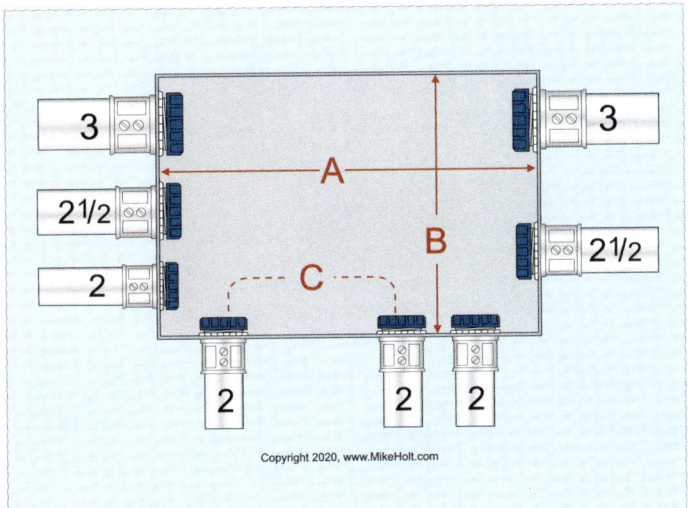

▶Figure 1

25. **(d) 24**
    314.28(A)(1)

    Straight:
    Left to Right = 8 × 3 in.
    Left to Right = 24 in.

    Right to Left = 8 × 3 in.
    Right to Left: = 24 in.

    Angle:
    Left to Right = (6 × 3 in.) +2.50 in. + 2
    Left to Right = 22.50 in.

    Right to Left = (6 × 3 in.) + 2.50 in.
    Right to Left = 20.50 in.

26. **(a) 16**
    314.28(A)(2)

    Straight = None possible.
    Top to Bottom: Angle = None possible.

    Bottom to Top: Angle = (6 × 2 in.) + 2 in. + 2 in.
    Bottom to Top: Angle = 16 in.

27. **(b) 4½**
    314.28(A)(2) Ex and Table 312.6(A)

Part 3 | Electrical Calculations Answer Key

Unit 6—Conductor Sizing and Protection

28. **(b) 12 AWG**

    310.15(B)(1)

    The conductor must have an ampacity of 16A at 90°C after applying the ambient temperature adjustment factor and it must be protected by a 20A protection device. Section 240.4(D) requires the conductor to be no smaller than 12 AWG.

    Conductor Required Ampacity = Load Amperes/Correction Factor

    Load Amperes = 20A

    Correction Factor for 90°C insulated conductor/ambient temperature at 120°F is 0.82 or 82%, Table 310.15(B)(1)

    Conductor Required Ampacity at 90°C = 20A/82%
    Conductor Required Ampacity at 90°C = 24.39A
    Conductor Required Ampacity at 90°C = 12 AWG rated 30A at 90°C, Table 310.16

29. **(b) 12**

    Corrected/Adjusted Ampacity = Table 310.16 × Correction 310.15(B)(1) × Adjustment Table 310.15(C)(1)

    Conductor Ampacity for 14 THHN is 25A at 90°C, Table 310.16
    Conductor Ampacity for 12 THHN is 30A at 90°C, Table 310.16
    Conductor Ampacity for 10 THHN is 40A at 90°C, Table 310.16
    Conductor Ampacity for 8 THHN is 55A at 90°C, Table 310.16

    Correction Factor for 90°C insulated conductor/ambient temperature at 75°F is 1.04 or 104%, Table 310.15(B)(1).

    Adjustment factor for nine current-carrying conductors is 70%, Table 310.15(C)(1).
    14 THHN Corrected/Adjusted Ampacity = 25A × 104% × 70% = 18.20A, cannot supply 19.70A load
    12 THHN Corrected/Adjusted Ampacity = 30A × 104% × 70% = 21.84A, can supply 19.70A load
    10 THHN Corrected/Adjusted Ampacity = 40A × 104% × 70% = 29.120A, can supply 19.70A load
    8 THHN Corrected/Adjusted Ampacity = 55A × 104% × 70% = 40.04A, can supply 19.70A load

30. **(c) 35A**

    310.15(C)(1)(b)

    Ampacity adjustment doesn't apply to raceways that are 24 in. in length or less.
    10 THW is rated 35A at 75°C, Table 310.16

31. **(c) 18.56A**

    Corrected/Adjusted Ampacity = Table 310.16 × Correction 310.15(B)(1) × Adjustment Table 310.15(C)(1)

    Conductor Ampacity for 10 THWN-2 is 40A at 90°C, Table 310.16
    Correction Factor for 90°C insulated conductor/ambient temperature at 94°F with a roof top adder of 60°F is 0.58 or 58%, Table 310.15(B)(1).
    Adjustment factor for four carrying conductors is 80%, Table 310.15(C)(1)

    Corrected/Adjusted Ampacity = 40A × 58% × 80%
    Corrected/Adjusted Ampacity = 18.56A

32. **(c) 9 conductors**

    310.15(E)(1) and 310.15(F)

    Current-Carrying Conductors

4-wire incandescent luminaires	3 conductors
4-wire fluorescent luminaires	4 conductors
2-wire receptacles	2 conductors
1 ground wire	+0 conductors
Total current-carrying	9 conductors

    Note: Electric-discharge lighting such as fluorescent lighting is a nonlinear load and produces harmonic currents, so the neutral is counted as current carrying (see the Note to the Article 100 definition of "nonlinear load."

33. (b) 7 conductors

    310.15(B)(1) and 310.15(F)

    Current-Carrying Conductors
4-wire incandescent luminaires	3 conductors
4-wire fluorescent luminaires	4 conductors
1 ground wire	+0 conductors
Total current-carrying	7 conductors

    Note: Electric-discharge lighting such as fluorescent lighting is a nonlinear load and produces harmonic currents, so the neutral is counted as current carrying (see the Note to the Article 100 definition of "nonlinear load."

34. (c) 60A

    The overcurrent protection device must be sized not less than 125% of the continuous load, 210.20(A), and 215.3.
    Overcurrent Protection = 45A × 125% (continuous load)
    Overcurrent Protection = 56.25A, round up to 60A, 240.6(A), 240.4(B)

35. (d) 600 kcmil

    Tap conductor not over 10 ft. long must have an ampacity no less than:

    - One-third of the rating of the 1,200A overcurrent device protecting the feeder conductors:
      1,200A × 33% = 400A, 600 kcmil rated 420A at 75°C, Table 310.16
    - The rating of the terminating 100A overcurrent device, 240.21(B)(2).
      225A Overcurrent Protection Device = 4/0 AWG rated 230A at 75°C, Table 310.16

Unit 7—Motor, Air-Conditioning, and Transformer Calculations

36. (a) 22A

    430.22(E)

    Table 430.22(E) Intermittent and 5-minute rated motor: The branch-circuit conductor ampacity must not be less than 85% of the motor nameplate amperes.

    Conductor = 25A × 85%
    Conductor = 21.25A
    10 AWG rated 30 at 60°C, 110.14(C)(1)(a)(2) and Table 310.16

37. (a) 1/0 AWG

    430.24(A)

    Motor FLC, Table 430.250
    50 hp = 65A
    20 hp = 27A
    10 hp = 14A

    Feeder conductor sized not less than 125% of largest motor FLC, plus FLCs of other motors, 430.24
    Feeder Conductor = (65A × 125%) +27A +14A +14A
    Feeder Conductor = 136A, 1/0 AWG rated 150A at 75°C, 110.14(C)(1)(b)(2) and Table 310.16

    Note: Duty cycle usage of a motor has no impact on feeder conductor sizing, only branch circuit conductor sizing.

38. (b) 24.70A

    430.32(A)(1)

    The motor overload for this motor must be sized no more than 115% of the motor nameplate current rating.

    Overload = 21.50A × 115%
    Overload = 24.73A

Part 3 | Electrical Calculations Answer Key

39. (c) 700A

430.52(C)(1) Ex 1

The branch-circuit protection device must not be greater than 150% of the motor FLC, Table 430.52

125 hp, 240V, dc motor FLC = 425A, Table 430.247

Branch Circuit Short-Circuit Ground-Fault Protection = 425A × 150%
Branch Circuit Short-Circuit Ground-Fault Protection = 637.50A, next size up 700A, 240.6(A) and 430.52(C)(1) Ex 1

40. (d) 90A

430.62(A)

To answer this question, the motors need to be distributed over the two phases; this results in only two motors per phase.

	Line 1	Line 2
Motor 1. 5 hp, 230V Motor	70A	70A
Motor 2. 1½ hp, 120V Motor	+20A	
Motor 3. 1½ hp, 120V Motor		+20A
Feeder Protection	90A	90A

The feeder protection device must not be greater than the largest branch-circuit protection device plus the sum of the motor FLCs on the same line. Largest branch-circuit protection device, 430.62(A):

5 hp, 230V, single phase motor FLC = 28A, Table 430.248

The branch-circuit protection device must not exceed 250% of the motor FLC:

Branch Circuit Short-Circuit Ground-Fault Protection = 28A × 250%
Branch Circuit Short-Circuit Ground-Fault Protection = 70A, 430.52(C)(1) and Table 430.52.

Feeder Protection not to Exceed = 70A +20A
Feeder Protection not to Exceed = 90A, 240.6(A)

Note: The service factor isn't used to size short-circuit and ground-fault protection for motor branch-circuits or feeders.

41. (d) all of these

Step 1: Determine the FLC, Table 430.250.

30 hp, 460V, three-phase synchronous motor = 32A (be sure to look in the synchronous motor section of the table)
10 hp, 460V, three-phase motor = 14A

Step 2: Determine the branch-circuit conductors, 430.22(a) and Table 310.16.

30 hp: 32A × 125% = 40A, 8 AWG rated 40A at 60°C, Table 310.16
10 hp: 14A × 125% = 18A, 12 AWG rated 20A at 60°C

Step 3: Determine the branch-circuit protection size 240.6(A), 430.52(C)(1) Ex 1, and Table 430.52:

30 hp: 32A × 250% = 80A
10 hp: 14A × 250% = 35A

Step 4: Determine the feeder conductor, 430.24.

Feeder Conductor = (32A × 125%) +14A
Feeder Conductor = 54A, 6 AWG rated 55A at 60°C, 110.14(C)(1)(a)(2) and Table 310.16

Step 5: Determine the feeder protection, 430.62:

The feeder protective device must not be greater than the largest branch-circuit device plus the sum of the FLCs on the same line.

Feeder Protection = Not greater than 80A +14A
Feeder Protection = Not greater than 94A, next size down 90A, 240.6(A) and 430.62(A)

42. (b) 175A

Annex D Example D8

43. **(b) 113,588 VA**

    VA Single Phase = Volts × Amperes

    VA Three Phase = Volts × 1.732 × Amperes

2 hp VA = 120V × 24A	2,880 VA
3 hp VA = 208V × 18.7A	3,890 VA
5 hp VA = 208V × 1.732 × 16.7A	6,016 VA
30 hp VA = 480V × 1.732 × 40A	33,254 VA
50 hp VA = 480V × 1.732 × 65A	54,038 VA
Largest Motor VA 25% Factor	+13,510 VA
Total VA	113,588 VA

44. **(d) 60A**

    Table 450.3(b) Note 1 next size up, 240.6(A)

    Primary Line Current = Primary Line Power/(Primary Line Voltage × 1.732)

    Primary Line Current = 37,500 VA/(480V × 1.732)

    Primary Line Current = 45.13A

    Overcurrent protection sized to Table 450.3(B): Not more than 125% of primary current

    Overcurrent Protection = 45.13A × 125%

    Overcurrent Protection = 56.41A, next size up 60A, 240.6(A)

Unit 8—Voltage-Drop Calculations

45. **(c) 0.05 ohms**

    Chapter 9, Table 9

    The ac resistance of 4 AWG aluminum conductors is 0.51 ohms in steel conduit for 1,000 ft

    R_{Total} = (Resistance/1000 ft) × Conductor Length

    R_{Total} = (0.51 ohms/1000 ft) × (2 wires × 50 ft)

    R_{Total} = 0.051 ohms

46. **(b) 6 AWG**

    No calculations are required for this problem. From Chapter 9, Table 9, the ac resistance of 4 AWG aluminum in a steel raceway (assumed) = 0.51ohms. 6 AWG copper in a steel raceway has an ac resistance of 0.49 ohms, Chapter 9, Table 9.

47. **(c) 232.80V**

    The *NEC* recommends a maximum 3% voltage drop on the branch-circuit conductors, which calculates out to be: 240V × 3% = 7.20V. The minimum voltage at the load is 240V less 7.20V = 232.80V or 240V × 97% = 232.80V.

48. **(b) 4.21V**

    VD = (2 × K × I × D)/Cmil

    K = 21.20 ohms, aluminum

    I = 55A (for voltage drop calculations, use the nameplate current rating, not the FLC rating)

    D = 95 ft

    Cmil = 3 AWG, 52,620 cmil, Chapter 9, Table 8

    VD = (2 conductors × 21.20 ohms × 55A × 95 ft)/52,620 cmil VD = 4.21V

Part 3 | Electrical Calculations Answer Key

49. (c) 339 ft

    D = (Cmil × VD Allowable)/(1.732 × K × I)

    Cmil = 52,620, Chapter 9, Table 8

    VD = 240V × 3% = 7.20V

    K = 12.90 ohms, copper

    I = 50A

    D = (52,620 cmil × 7.20V)/(1.732 × 12.90 ohms × 50A)
    D = 339 ft

50. (c) 10A

    I = (Cmil × VD Allowable)/(2 × K × D)

    Cmil = 16,510, Chapter 9, Table 8

    VD = 120V × 3%
    VD = 3.60V

    K = 12.90 ohms, copper

    D = 225 ft

    I = (16,510 cmil × 3.60V)/(2 conductors × 12.90 ohms × 225 ft)
    I = 10A

Unit 9—Dwelling Unit Calculations

51. (c) 125A

220.82(B)

Step 1: Determine the total connected load.

General Lighting	1,800 sq ft × 3 VA	5,400 VA
Small-Appliance Circuits	1,500 VA × 2 circuits	3,000 VA
Laundry Circuit		1,500 VA
Dishwasher		1,500 VA
Disposal		1,000 VA
Water Heater		4,000 W
Dryer		4,500 W
Cooktop		6,000 W
Ovens	3,000 W × 2	6,000 W
Pool Pump		1,600 VA
Total Connected Load		34,500 VA

Step 2: Determine demand load for Step 1 load.

Total Connected Load	34,500 VA	
First 10,000 at 100%	-10,000 VA × 100% =	10,000 VA
Remainder at 40%	24,500 VA × 40% =	+9,800 VA
Total Demand Load		19,800 VA

Step 3: Determine larger of air-conditioning 100% versus space heating at 40%

Air Conditioner VA = Volts × Amperes

Air Conditioner VA = 240V × 28A
Air Conditioner VA = 6,720 VA at 100%

Space Heating at 40%

Space Heating = 2 kW × 5 units × 40%
Space Heating = 4,000 W, omit 220.82(5)

Step 4: Determine service size.

Demand Load from Step: 2	19,800 VA
Demand Load from Step: 3	+6,720 VA
Total Demand Load	26,520 VA

Service Size in Amperes = VA Demand Load/System Volts

I = 26,520 VA/240V
I = 111A, 125 Service, 240.6(A)

Feeder/Service Conductors; 2 AWG copper or 1/0 AWG aluminum, Table 310.12

52. (b) 4,800 VA

220.82(C)(1) & (5)

The larger of the Air Conditioner at 100% versus Space Heating at 40%.

Air Conditioner Load at 100%

Air Conditioner VA = 240V × 20A
Air Conditioner VA = 4,800 VA × 100%

Space Heating Load at 40%

Space Heating = 2 kW × 5 units × 40%
Space Heating = 4,000 W omit

Larger Air Conditioner VA = 4,800 VA

Part 3 | Electrical Calculations Answer Key

53. **(b) 109A**
    220.82(C)(1) & (4)

    Step 1: Determine the total connected load, 220.82.

General Lighting	2,200 sq ft. × 3 VA	6,600 VA
Small-Appliance Circuits	1,500 VA × 2 circuits	3,000 VA
Laundry Circuit		1,500 VA
Dishwasher		1,200 VA
Disposal	Rated 120V × 8A	960 VA
Attic Fan	Rated 120V × 16A	1,920 VA
Water Heater		4,500 W
Dryer		5,000 W
Range		+14,000 W
Total Connected Load		38,680 VA

    Step 2: Determine the Step 1 demand load.

Total Connected Load	38,680 VA	
First 10 kW at 100%	−10,000 VA × 100% =	10,000 VA
Remainder at 40%	28,680 VA × 40% =	+11,472 VA
Step 1 Demand Load		21,472 VA

    Step 3: Determine the larger of air-conditioning 100% versus space heating at 65%

    Air Conditioner Load at 100%
    Air Conditioner VA = 240V × 10A
    Air Conditioner VA = (2,400 VA × 2 units) × 100%
    Air Conditioner VA = 4,800 VA

    Space Heating = 6,000 W at 65%
    Space Heating = 3,900 W, omit 220.60

    Step 4: Determine total demand load.

Step 2. Total	21,472 VA
Step 3. Total	+4,800 W
Total	26,272 VA

    Step 5: Determine service size in amperes.

    Service Size in Amperes = VA Demand Load/System Volts
    I = 26,272 VA/240V
    I = 109A

54. **(d) 5.50 kW**
    220.54

    Use a minimum of 5 kW or the nameplate rating, whichever is larger.

55. **(c) 7.80 kW**
    Table 220.55 Note 3

    Step 1: Determine the total connected load: 6 kW +6 kW = 12 kW.

    Step 2: Column B demand factor for two units: 65%.

    Step 3: Apply the Column B demand factor to the total connected load: 12 kW × 65% = 7.80 kW.

56. (b) 9.30 kW

    Table 220.55 Note 3

    Table 220.55 Note 3 permits Column A and Column B demand factors to be used.

    Step 1: Determine the total connected load.

    Column A = 3 kW +3 kW
    Column A = 6 kW
    Column B = 6 kW

    Step 2: Determine the Column A and Column B demand factors:

    Column A (two units) = 75%
    Column B (one unit) = 80%

    Step 3: Determine the Column A demand factor: 6 kW × 75% = 4.50 kW

    Column B Demand Factor = 6 kW × 80%
    Column B Demand Factor = 4.80 kW

    Total Demand Load = 4.50 kW +4.80 kW
    Total Demand Load = 9.30 kW

57. (d) 17 kW

    Table 220.55 Note 3

    Table 220.55 Note 3 lets us use Column B or A "in lieu of" Column C, but the answer will always be the smaller of Table 220.55 Column B versus Column C.

    Table 220.55 Column B
    Column B = (6 kW × 2) +3.50 kW +(8 kW × 3) × 43%
    Column B = 12 kW +3.50 kW +24 kW × 43%
    Column B = 39.50 kW × 43%
    Column B = 17 kW

    Table 220.55 Column C, six units = 21 kW

58. (d) 8 kW

    Table 220.55 Note 4

    Treat as a single 12 kW range = 8 kW Column C

Part 3 | Electrical Calculations Answer Key

59. (b) 133A

Step 1: Determine the lighting and Receptacles, 220.42.

General Lighting	2,200 sq. ft × 3 VA per sq. ft	6,600 VA
Small-Appliance Circuits	1,500 VA × 2 circuits	3,000 VA
Laundry Circuit		+1,500 VA
Total Connected Load		11,100 VA
First 3,000 VA at 100%		−3,000 VA × 100% = 3,000 VA
Remainder VA at 35%		8,100 VA × 35% = +2,835 VA
Total General Lighting and Receptacle Load		5,835 VA

Step 2: Determine the appliances, 220.53.

Dishwasher	1,200 VA	
Disposal 120V × 9.80A	1,176 VA	
Microwave	1,920 VA	
Water Heater	4,200 W	
Total Connected Appliance Load	+8,496 VA	
Total Demand Load	8,496 VA × 75% =	6,372 VA

Step 3: Determine the dryer, 220.54 minimum: 5,000 W.

Step 4: The Column C value (8 kW) must be increased 5% for each kW or major fraction of a kW over 12 kW, 220.55 Note 1. The 14 kW range exceeds 12 kW by 2 kW. Column C value must be increased by 2 × 5% = 10%.

Demand Load = Column C Value × Table 220.55 Note 1 Multiplier
Demand Load = 8 kW × 110%
Demand Load = 8.80 kW or 8,800 W

Step 5: Determine the air conditioner versus heat.

Air Conditioner two units each rated 12A at 120V.

VA = Volts × Amperes
Air Conditioner VA = 120V × 12A
Air Conditioner VA = 1,440 VA
Air Conditioner VA = (1,440 VA × 125%) + 1,440 VA
Air Conditioner VA = 3,168 VA, omit 220.60

Space Heating = 6,000 W

Step 6: Determine the service load totals.

Step 1. Lighting and Receptacles	5,835 VA
Step 2. Appliances	6,372 VA
Step 3. Dryer	5,000 W
Step 4. Range	8,800 W
Step 5. Space Heating	+6,000 W
Total Demand Load	32,007 VA

Service Size in Amperes = VA Demand Load/System Volts
I = 32,007 VA/240
I = 133A

60. (a) 58A

Step 1: Determine the lighting and receptacles, 220.42.

General Lighting	950 sq. ft × 3 VA per sq. ft	2,850 VA
Small-Appliance Circuits	1,500 VA × 2 circuits	3,000 VA
Laundry Circuit		+1,500 VA
Total Connected Load		7,350 VA
First 3,000 VA at 100%	−3,000 VA × 100% =	3,000 VA
Remainder VA at 35%	4,350 VA × 35% =	+1,523 VA
Total General Lighting and Receptacle Load		4,523 VA

Step 2: Determine the appliances, 220.53.

Dishwasher rated 12A at 120V = 1,440 VA

Step 3: Determine the dryer, 220.54, minimum.

5,000 W × 70% = 3,500 W

Step 4: Determine the cooking equipment, 220.55 Note 3, Column B: 8,000 W × 80% = 6,400 W × 70% = 4,480 VA

Step 6: Determine the service load totals.

Lighting and Receptacles	4,523 VA
Appliances	1,440 VA
Dryer	3,500 W
Range	+4,480 W
Total Neutral Demand Load	13,943 VA

Service Neutral Amperes = Neutral Demand Load/System Volts

I = 13,943 VA/240V

I = 58A

Notes

PART 1

ELECTRICAL THEORY ANSWER SHEET

1. (a) (b) (c) (d)
2. (a) (b) (c) (d)
3. (a) (b) (c) (d)
4. (a) (b) (c) (d)
5. (a) (b) (c) (d)
6. (a) (b) (c) (d)
7. (a) (b) (c) (d)
8. (a) (b) (c) (d)
9. (a) (b) (c) (d)
10. (a) (b) (c) (d)
11. (a) (b) (c) (d)
12. (a) (b) (c) (d)
13. (a) (b) (c) (d)
14. (a) (b) (c) (d)
15. (a) (b) (c) (d)
16. (a) (b) (c) (d)
17. (a) (b) (c) (d)
18. (a) (b) (c) (d)
19. (a) (b) (c) (d)
20. (a) (b) (c) (d)
21. (a) (b) (c) (d)
22. (a) (b) (c) (d)
23. (a) (b) (c) (d)
24. (a) (b) (c) (d)
25. (a) (b) (c) (d)
26. (a) (b) (c) (d)
27. (a) (b) (c) (d)
28. (a) (b) (c) (d)
29. (a) (b) (c) (d)
30. (a) (b) (c) (d)
31. (a) (b) (c) (d)
32. (a) (b) (c) (d)
33. (a) (b) (c) (d)
34. (a) (b) (c) (d)
35. (a) (b) (c) (d)
36. (a) (b) (c) (d)
37. (a) (b) (c) (d)
38. (a) (b) (c) (d)
39. (a) (b) (c) (d)
40. (a) (b) (c) (d)
41. (a) (b) (c) (d)
42. (a) (b) (c) (d)
43. (a) (b) (c) (d)
44. (a) (b) (c) (d)
45. (a) (b) (c) (d)
46. (a) (b) (c) (d)
47. (a) (b) (c) (d)
48. (a) (b) (c) (d)
49. (a) (b) (c) (d)
50. (a) (b) (c) (d)
51. (a) (b) (c) (d)
52. (a) (b) (c) (d)
53. (a) (b) (c) (d)
54. (a) (b) (c) (d)
55. (a) (b) (c) (d)
56. (a) (b) (c) (d)
57. (a) (b) (c) (d)
58. (a) (b) (c) (d)
59. (a) (b) (c) (d)
60. (a) (b) (c) (d)
61. (a) (b) (c) (d)
62. (a) (b) (c) (d)
63. (a) (b) (c) (d)
64. (a) (b) (c) (d)
65. (a) (b) (c) (d)
66. (a) (b) (c) (d)
67. (a) (b) (c) (d)
68. (a) (b) (c) (d)
69. (a) (b) (c) (d)
70. (a) (b) (c) (d)
71. (a) (b) (c) (d)
72. (a) (b) (c) (d)
73. (a) (b) (c) (d)
74. (a) (b) (c) (d)
75. (a) (b) (c) (d)
76. (a) (b) (c) (d)
77. (a) (b) (c) (d)
78. (a) (b) (c) (d)
79. (a) (b) (c) (d)
80. (a) (b) (c) (d)
81. (a) (b) (c) (d)
82. (a) (b) (c) (d)
83. (a) (b) (c) (d)
84. (a) (b) (c) (d)
85. (a) (b) (c) (d)
86. (a) (b) (c) (d)
87. (a) (b) (c) (d)
88. (a) (b) (c) (d)
89. (a) (b) (c) (d)
90. (a) (b) (c) (d)
91. (a) (b) (c) (d)
92. (a) (b) (c) (d)
93. (a) (b) (c) (d)
94. (a) (b) (c) (d)
95. (a) (b) (c) (d)
96. (a) (b) (c) (d)
97. (a) (b) (c) (d)
98. (a) (b) (c) (d)
99. (a) (b) (c) (d)
100. (a) (b) (c) (d)

Notes

PART 2

NATIONAL ELECTRICAL CODE ANSWER SHEET

1. (a) (b) (c) (d)
2. (a) (b) (c) (d)
3. (a) (b) (c) (d)
4. (a) (b) (c) (d)
5. (a) (b) (c) (d)
6. (a) (b) (c) (d)
7. (a) (b) (c) (d)
8. (a) (b) (c) (d)
9. (a) (b) (c) (d)
10. (a) (b) (c) (d)
11. (a) (b) (c) (d)
12. (a) (b) (c) (d)
13. (a) (b) (c) (d)
14. (a) (b) (c) (d)
15. (a) (b) (c) (d)
16. (a) (b) (c) (d)
17. (a) (b) (c) (d)
18. (a) (b) (c) (d)
19. (a) (b) (c) (d)
20. (a) (b) (c) (d)
21. (a) (b) (c) (d)
22. (a) (b) (c) (d)
23. (a) (b) (c) (d)
24. (a) (b) (c) (d)
25. (a) (b) (c) (d)
26. (a) (b) (c) (d)
27. (a) (b) (c) (d)
28. (a) (b) (c) (d)
29. (a) (b) (c) (d)
30. (a) (b) (c) (d)
31. (a) (b) (c) (d)
32. (a) (b) (c) (d)
33. (a) (b) (c) (d)
34. (a) (b) (c) (d)
35. (a) (b) (c) (d)
36. (a) (b) (c) (d)
37. (a) (b) (c) (d)
38. (a) (b) (c) (d)
39. (a) (b) (c) (d)
40. (a) (b) (c) (d)
41. (a) (b) (c) (d)
42. (a) (b) (c) (d)
43. (a) (b) (c) (d)
44. (a) (b) (c) (d)
45. (a) (b) (c) (d)
46. (a) (b) (c) (d)
47. (a) (b) (c) (d)
48. (a) (b) (c) (d)
49. (a) (b) (c) (d)
50. (a) (b) (c) (d)
51. (a) (b) (c) (d)
52. (a) (b) (c) (d)
53. (a) (b) (c) (d)
54. (a) (b) (c) (d)
55. (a) (b) (c) (d)
56. (a) (b) (c) (d)
57. (a) (b) (c) (d)
58. (a) (b) (c) (d)
59. (a) (b) (c) (d)
60. (a) (b) (c) (d)
61. (a) (b) (c) (d)
62. (a) (b) (c) (d)
63. (a) (b) (c) (d)
64. (a) (b) (c) (d)
65. (a) (b) (c) (d)
66. (a) (b) (c) (d)
67. (a) (b) (c) (d)
68. (a) (b) (c) (d)
69. (a) (b) (c) (d)
70. (a) (b) (c) (d)
71. (a) (b) (c) (d)
72. (a) (b) (c) (d)
73. (a) (b) (c) (d)
74. (a) (b) (c) (d)
75. (a) (b) (c) (d)
76. (a) (b) (c) (d)
77. (a) (b) (c) (d)
78. (a) (b) (c) (d)
79. (a) (b) (c) (d)
80. (a) (b) (c) (d)
81. (a) (b) (c) (d)
82. (a) (b) (c) (d)
83. (a) (b) (c) (d)
84. (a) (b) (c) (d)
85. (a) (b) (c) (d)
86. (a) (b) (c) (d)
87. (a) (b) (c) (d)
88. (a) (b) (c) (d)
89. (a) (b) (c) (d)
90. (a) (b) (c) (d)
91. (a) (b) (c) (d)
92. (a) (b) (c) (d)
93. (a) (b) (c) (d)
94. (a) (b) (c) (d)
95. (a) (b) (c) (d)
96. (a) (b) (c) (d)
97. (a) (b) (c) (d)
98. (a) (b) (c) (d)
99. (a) (b) (c) (d)
100. (a) (b) (c) (d)

Notes

PART 3
ELECTRICAL CALCULATIONS ANSWER SHEET

1. ⓐ ⓑ ⓒ ⓓ
2. ⓐ ⓑ ⓒ ⓓ
3. ⓐ ⓑ ⓒ ⓓ
4. ⓐ ⓑ ⓒ ⓓ
5. ⓐ ⓑ ⓒ ⓓ
6. ⓐ ⓑ ⓒ ⓓ
7. ⓐ ⓑ ⓒ ⓓ
8. ⓐ ⓑ ⓒ ⓓ
9. ⓐ ⓑ ⓒ ⓓ
10. ⓐ ⓑ ⓒ ⓓ
11. ⓐ ⓑ ⓒ ⓓ
12. ⓐ ⓑ ⓒ ⓓ
13. ⓐ ⓑ ⓒ ⓓ
14. ⓐ ⓑ ⓒ ⓓ
15. ⓐ ⓑ ⓒ ⓓ
16. ⓐ ⓑ ⓒ ⓓ
17. ⓐ ⓑ ⓒ ⓓ
18. ⓐ ⓑ ⓒ ⓓ
19. ⓐ ⓑ ⓒ ⓓ
20. ⓐ ⓑ ⓒ ⓓ
21. ⓐ ⓑ ⓒ ⓓ
22. ⓐ ⓑ ⓒ ⓓ
23. ⓐ ⓑ ⓒ ⓓ
24. ⓐ ⓑ ⓒ ⓓ
25. ⓐ ⓑ ⓒ ⓓ
26. ⓐ ⓑ ⓒ ⓓ
27. ⓐ ⓑ ⓒ ⓓ
28. ⓐ ⓑ ⓒ ⓓ
29. ⓐ ⓑ ⓒ ⓓ
30. ⓐ ⓑ ⓒ ⓓ
31. ⓐ ⓑ ⓒ ⓓ
32. ⓐ ⓑ ⓒ ⓓ
33. ⓐ ⓑ ⓒ ⓓ
34. ⓐ ⓑ ⓒ ⓓ
35. ⓐ ⓑ ⓒ ⓓ
36. ⓐ ⓑ ⓒ ⓓ
37. ⓐ ⓑ ⓒ ⓓ
38. ⓐ ⓑ ⓒ ⓓ
39. ⓐ ⓑ ⓒ ⓓ
40. ⓐ ⓑ ⓒ ⓓ
41. ⓐ ⓑ ⓒ ⓓ
42. ⓐ ⓑ ⓒ ⓓ
43. ⓐ ⓑ ⓒ ⓓ
44. ⓐ ⓑ ⓒ ⓓ
45. ⓐ ⓑ ⓒ ⓓ
46. ⓐ ⓑ ⓒ ⓓ
47. ⓐ ⓑ ⓒ ⓓ
48. ⓐ ⓑ ⓒ ⓓ
49. ⓐ ⓑ ⓒ ⓓ
50. ⓐ ⓑ ⓒ ⓓ
51. ⓐ ⓑ ⓒ ⓓ
52. ⓐ ⓑ ⓒ ⓓ
53. ⓐ ⓑ ⓒ ⓓ
54. ⓐ ⓑ ⓒ ⓓ
55. ⓐ ⓑ ⓒ ⓓ
56. ⓐ ⓑ ⓒ ⓓ
57. ⓐ ⓑ ⓒ ⓓ
58. ⓐ ⓑ ⓒ ⓓ
59. ⓐ ⓑ ⓒ ⓓ
60. ⓐ ⓑ ⓒ ⓓ

Notes